INTERNATIONAL ECONOMIC

INTEGRATION

DISTRIBUTORS FOR
THE BRITISH COMMONWEALTH AND THE U.S.A.:
CLEAVER-HUME PRESS LTD.
31 WRIGHT'S LANE, KENSINGTON, LONDON, W.8

INTERNATIONAL ECONOMIC

INTEGRATION

SECOND, COMPLETELY REVISED, EDITION OF
INTERNATIONAL ECONOMIC CO-OPERATION

by

J. TINBERGEN

Professor of Econometrics, Netherlands School of Economics

AMSTERDAM ELSEVIER BRUSSELS

MCMLIV

PRINTED IN THE NETHERLANDS BY
DRUKKERIJ MEIJER, WORMERVEER AND AMSTERDAM

PREFACE

This book in a way constitutes a second edition of my
'International Economic Co-operation', published 1945.
It has been completely re-written, however, in order to
take account of the rapid development in thinking as well
as in international economic co-operation itself. As the
change in title indicates the emphasis has also been slightly
shifted: the process of integration has been chosen as the
aim towards which the analysis is directed.

The booklet is meant, as in its first edition, for those not
officially trained or not yet trained in economics and tries
to stick to simple language. Nevertheless it tries to con-
centrate on the economic background of the integration
process rather than on events or documentation: economic
reasoning is its main instrument. In two appendices the
foundations of this reasoning are exemplified in some more
detail.

My sincere thanks are due to Mr. M. A. M. G. van
Beusekom, who revised the idiom.

J. T.

CONTENTS

FIRST PART. THE ESSENCE OF INTERNATIONAL ECO-
NOMIC RELATIONS BETWEEN AUTONOMOUS
NATIONS

CHAPTER I. *Introduction; the Heterogeneity of World Economy*

1.1. This book is written for the general public interested in problems of international economic co-operation, not for specialists. Its two Parts try to give, respectively, an insight into the nature of international economic relations in a world of autonomous governments, and into the question in what respect these relations should be deliberately regulated in an 'integrated' world.

1.2. The world economy consists of a great number of national economies, which in some respects are almost watertight compartments, but in other respects are narrowly connected. There is a considerable difference in *population* and in *wealth* between the national economies. This wealth consists of natural resources and capital goods; some figures.

1.3. Areas of different structure distinguished by Wagemann.

1.4. In each of the national economies goods and services are produced with the help of the three so-called *factors of production:* nature or land, labour and capital.

1.5. *Production per head* depends on the quantities of land and of capital available per head, of the quality of the population and on the institutional framework in which production is organized.

1.6. Hence the great differences in *prosperity*. China and India are the principal underdeveloped areas of the world. The total product is divided among the factors labour, land and capital in proportion which, curiously enough, do not greatly vary for different countries; broadly speaking they are 70, 10 and 20%.

1.7. There are the following possibilities of economic intercourse between nations;

(1) Transfer of *products:* mainly against other products in the form of current trade; incidentally in the form of gifts or other unilateral transfers;

(2) Transfer of *factors of production:*
   (a) persons: migration;
   (b) land: change of territory;
   (c) capital: capital imports and exports.

Transfer (2b) is not frequent; it may occur as a consequence of political events. In the interwar period (2a) did not occur frequently either; by far the most important forms of intercourse are, therefore, (1) and (2c).

Chapter II. *Current Transactions*

II.1. Current transactions between countries are those in products, i.e. goods and services, excluding those in factors of production. Each country will export products which it is able to produce at lower cost than other countries. Low-price products not likely to move over long distances. Large countries likely to have a smaller percentage of foreign trade than small countries.

The structure of commercial transactions between four broad subdivisions of the world: surpluses and deficits.

II.2. Generally transactions will be *multilateral*. Distinction between (i) net surplus or deficit for any country, (ii) bilateral, (iii) circular and (iv) open flow component. In a situation of equilibrium (i) does not exist; for the world at large (iv) cannot exist.

II.3. Trade may be (i) *free*, (ii) *hampered* more or less arbitrarily or (iii) *controlled*. Trade may be hampered by quantitative restrictions, currency restrictions or import duties. There may be blocks of countries with free internal trade, and with a common tariff for the outside world *(customs unions)* or even groups of countries with completely free trade *(free trade areas)*. We speak of *integration* or an economic union if also other aspects of economic policy are unified so as to present an optimum of centralization.

II.4. With *free trade*, prices of international goods are — apart from transportation costs — uniform throughout the world; and trade will be multilateral. Even with free trade there may be *imperfect competition*, e.g. because of distances. The short-term elasticity of the share of any one country in world trade with respect to its relative price level appears to be no more than 2. The short-term elasticity of import quotas appears to be also rather restricted. Probably long-term elasticities are higher.

II.5. International trade as a consequence of differences between countries in relative efficiency in producing various commodities *(theory of comparative cost)*. Differences in standard of living as a consequence of differences in efficiency in producing all or most commodities.

II.6. *The fundamental thesis of the doctrine of free trade:* With full employment of all resources and marginal cost pricing free trade yields — in the long run — a maximum of total production and hence, apart form certain questions of distribution, a maximum of welfare. Every deviation from it therefore means, for small countries, a smaller prosperity; it can only be an advantage for some groups within those countries at the expense of other groups in the same countries. Large countries may, by tariff policy, improve their terms of trade and their real expenditure. Marginal cost pricing may not be possible in certain industries without subsidizing them. Subsidies to be preferred to protection. Without full employment being guaranteed beforehand protection may, in some country, cause an increase in employment and therefore raise prosperity. The maintenance of full employment requires a compensatory financial policy.

II.7. Protection may help to break the shock of a *sudden adaptation* to new circumstances or to stimulate infant industries. The danger of protection is in the possible maintenance of less productive units.

II.8. Liberalization of trade generally will also mean the disruption of bilateral equilibria; it can only be performed therefore if at the same time a certain convertibility of currencies is re-established.

II.9. Customs unions may, but need not, be a step towards world free trade: '*trade divertion*' versus '*trade creation*' (VINER).

CHAPTER III. *International Movements of Factors: Land, Labour and Capital*

III.1. Movements of *land* in the literal sense are of course impossible. The transfer of territory from one nation to another may, however, be considered as an example. So far such a transfer has not been considered a possible element of economic policy.

III.2. Movements of labour, i.e. of *population*, or migration, have been important for the areas of immigration, such as the United States of America, but as a rule only of minor significance to the areas of emigration. After 1914 the extent of migratory movements has been very restricted. It is to be hoped that, under certain guarantees, the less populated countries will be prepared to revise their policies.

III.3. From the economic point of view *capital* movements represent by far the most important form of international movements of factors of production. It may take the form of loans in the narrower sense or of participation; loans may be short-term or long-term loans. Long-term loans (in the wider sense, i.e. including participation) come down, in real terms, to the transfer of commodity stocks (durable and non-durable goods) from the lending to the borrowing area at the price of an annual 'mortgage' on part of the latter's production. Usually the lending area will be one of the highly developed countries and the borrowing area one of the under-developed countries, where the marginal productivity of capital will be higher. In this way a decrease in the inequality in living conditions may be obtained. So far, however, the divergency in living conditions between developed and underdeveloped countries has increased. Hindrances to capital movements are to be found in uncertain political conditions, unstable financial and monetary conditions, or low efficiency of production. The vicious circle of low productivity for lack of external economies and low capital formation; its possible break by an international investment policy.

III.4. Short-term capital movements are of much less direct significance for the trend of development but may contribute to the maintenance of financial stability and hence contribute indirectly to development.

CHAPTER IV. *The Mechanism of Financial Transactions*

IV.1. Only *gold* is legal tender everywhere; as payment in gold involves high costs, other means of payment have developed, namely paper money, the value of which is based on law and confidence and is therefore restricted to a certain area. Payment to foreign countries therefore requires a '*transfer*', i.e. a transformation of home into foreign currency. This is effectuated by exchanging the various currencies against each other at a certain market price (the *rate of exchange*).

IV.2. The set of all payments made in a certain period between a country and all other countries is called its *balance of payments*. It may be subdivided into the *current items* (balance of trade, or imports and exports of goods; and invisible imports and exports or payments for services: shipping, interest, tourism etc.) and the *capital items* (import and export of capital: long-term and short-term; and the balancing item of gold shipments). In addition *unilateral payments* may occur in the balance of payments, as e.g. foreign aid and reparation payments.

IV.3. If the equilibrating item is included, there is always equilibrium (*formal* equilibrium); if it is not included, the phrase 'the balance of payments' has a different meaning. It may or may not be in equilibrium (*material* equilibrium). In the long run there must be material equilibrium, otherwise there would be a permanent accumulation of gold somewhere and a permanent drain elsewhere. A modest drain may, however, be a permanent phenomenon. Long-run material equilibrium must also exist, and for similar reasons, for any part of a currency area.

IV.4. *Stability of exchange rates* is an advantage for economic calculations, but it may be non-compatible with stable prices, which are desirable for other reasons. Usually fixed rates, with incidental revisions, are preferred. With the '*gold standard*', there is a fixed price in each country against which the Central Bank buys or sells gold. The corresponding rate of exchange is called the *parity rate*. At both sides of parity there are rates called the '*gold points*', indicating the limits within which gold shipments are unremunerative. Only a rigorous material equilibrium in the balance of payments will keep the exchange rates between the gold points. If one of the gold points is reached, a movement of gold will follow, tending to keep the rate of exchange at that point. If it should go on for some time there is the threat of an exhaustion of the gold stock of one of the countries concerned. This can be prevented by (a) 'indirect' or (b) ' direct' action.

IV.5. Indirect action may be (1) automatic, resulting from the changes in the monetary circulation: a decrease in gold stock leading to a decrease in note circulation or deposits, a reduction in incomes and hence reduced imports and lower prices which will stimulate exports. This automatism does not, however, work very strongly and quickly. Indirect action may also be (2) deliberate interference, namely a *raising of the rate of discount* in the threatened country, owing to which partly the same results are obtained (though again only weakly and slowly), and partly more important changes, namely an inflow of short-term credits from abroad — provided there are no counteracting factors such as lack of confidence. This remedy can, however, only work temporarily: after some time a new equilibrium in the capital market will be reached. The 'defence of the Dutch guilder' during 1935/6.

IV.6. Direct action is equivalent to *stopping the sale of gold;* this means either the end of the free gold standard or of the previous parity. The old parity may be maintained at the cost of freedom. Of course, the danger of an exhaustion of the gold stock is smallest when a country has a large gold reserve.

IV.7. Apart from gold a country's currency system may be based upon (1) other currencies (gold exchange standard) or (2) other commodities (silver, raw materials). Consequences of a *raw material standard:* stabilization of the average price level of raw materials and reduction of cyclic movements as far as due to 'accounting errors' in income determination.

IV.8. In principle, the system of *flexible rates* operates in the same way as the gold standard. The limits between which the

13

rate of exchange is allowed to fluctuate can be chosen wider or narrower. Smaller fluctuations may be counteracted by the operations of an *equalization fund*. In the longer run, changes in the rate of exchange will be helpful to equilibrate the balance of payments, since they affect imports and exports via the price system. By only permitting gradual movements the influence of speculation may be kept down, which proved disastrous in a number of cases (Germany 1923).

Chapter V. *Disequilibrium and Equilibrium in the Balance of Payments*

v.1. In this chapter some consequences of disequilibrium will be considered; the conditions for equilibrium will be formulated and some techniques of short-term adaptation discussed. With multilateral equilibrium, i.e. equilibrium in the balances of payments of all countries, there will be the possibility of *complete convertibility*.

v.2. If not every balance of payments is in equilibrium there will be deficit and surplus countries. The currency reserves of the deficit countries will gradually diminish. Once they are exhausted the currency of the country will be inconvertible or a '*soft currency*' as distinguished from '*hard*' *currencies*. The 'degree of softness'.

v.3. *Partial convertibility* may be instituted by decree, but can only be maintained if the country concerned is near to the equilibrium position which is relevant to the type of convertibility considered. It may bear on convertibility into some other currency, or for certain types of transactions. Convertibility with respect to current transactions with a given group of other countries requires that the total of these transactions — under the new circumstances — be in equilibrium. The 'new circumstances' imply the shifts in transactions as a consequence of convertibility itself.

v.4. Detailed examination of consequences.

v.5. Convertibility for all transactions, including *capital transactions*, is exposed to far greater risks, because of the incalculability of switches in capital assets that the public may desire. Example of the British convertibility attempt in 1947. Convertibility of currency A into currency B and of B into C has to imply convertibility of A into C also; there have to be groups of mutually convertible currencies, consisting of currencies of about equal strength.

v.6. Equivalence, for small countries, of *balance of payments equilibrium* and *monetary equilibrium;* inflationary and deflationary gap. Meaning of monetary equilibrium for small and for large countries. Regulation of national expenditure and of the price level needed in order to maintain balance of payments equilibrium at a level of high and stable employment.

v.7. Equilibrium, just described, to be understood as one *relatively to other countries.* Possibility of world inflation. '*Imported*' inflation and '*exported*' inflation.

v.8. In order to attain or to maintain equilibrium in the balances of payments various instruments are available.

A distinction may be made between:

(1) autonomous *changes in quantities demanded*, without changes in price ratios or absolute prices; and

v.9. (2) *changes in price ratios*, inducing changes in quantities, and themselves to be obtained by: (i) direct changes in absolute prices; (ii) indirect changes, i.e. changes in wage levels or rates of exchange.

A closer examination teaches that:

(A) sometimes price ratios need not be changed, if the automatic quantitative reactions upon the disturbing forces restore equilibrium already;

v.10. (B) in other cases price ratio changes do not work (the case of the *critical* or nearly critical *elasticities* of imports and exports);

(C) in still other cases price changes do work, but cannot be obtained by changes in wage or exchange rates (the case of purely static reactions);

(D) and hence price ratio changes, when necessary, can be obtained by wage or exchange rate policy only under certain conditions.

In case B, autonomous changes in quantities demanded (such as an 'austerity policy' or continued imports of capital or the cancellation of debts) are the only way out; in case C either direct price policy or autonomous changes in quantities will be necessary.

SECOND PART

INTERNATIONAL ECONOMIC INTEGRATION

CHAPTER VI. *Targets and Instruments of International Economic Integration*

VI.1. After having dealt with the nature of international economic relations between autonomous nations and the possibilities to regulate them, we shall now discuss how far we want to regulate them, or in modern terms, how far we want to *integrate* the various national economies. This problem of integration has to be seen as a part of the more general problem of the *optimum economic policy*. When making recommendations of economic policy we are to some extent leaving the territory of economic science. We shall be careful to warn the reader each time we do so.

VI.2. It is useful, in order to clarify problems of economic policy, to distinguish between *qualitative* and *quantitative* policy; qualitative policy being a change in organization and quantitative policy a change, within a given frame of organization, of certain data to be called *instruments*. Changes in organization may be of a very fundamental character and then be called reforms or even revolutions; or they may be changes in details of organization. Quantitative policies may either use numerous or a small number of instruments, and a distinction may be made between direct and indirect policies, where the former directly interfere with market forces and the latter only indirectly.

VI.3. An important aspect of qualitative changes in policy is the one of *centralization* or *decentralization*, especially in international affairs.

VI.4. Directives for the desirable degree of centralization in international economic policy: decentralization of *neutral*, or almost neutral, instruments and centralization of clearly *supporting* and clearly *conflicting* instruments.

VI.5. The choice of a policy has to depend on circumstances and will, in addition, be a question of taste. Necessity of a policy of intervention in cases of serious disturbances or of serious emergencies. Difference in tastes and pre-conceived ideas also determine the choice of instruments. Examples.

VI.6 The *aims* of economic policy cannot be formulated on the basis of economic science alone. Welfare dependent on individual wellbeing and the relations to other individuals. Incomparability of satisfaction of different individuals and the resulting difficulties. Almost generally accepted aims are those of *high production* and of a *more equal distribution* in case of strong inequality. High production requires the *use of all productive resources* (implying avoidance of instability) and the use of these resources in the *most efficient* way. The use of instruments of detailed intervention should be restricted to the *prevention of strong disequilibria*.

VI.7. The differences in economic policy between the communist and the non-communist countries may partly be explained by circumstances. They are strong enough to make it impossible to aim at one world policy. International relations with communist

16

countries have to be highly centralized. Only relations between non-communist countries may be adapted to what we consider an optimum degree of centralization.

vi.8. Problem of integration to be studied, in succession, for national instruments and for international instruments of economic policy.

CHAPTER VII. *National Economic Policies and International Integration*

vii.1. Since the basic circumstances may be different from country to country economic policy or even the basic organization of economic life may be widely different. As far as centrally organized or highly interventionist, countries may accordingly organize their international relations. Less strongly centralized countries will prefer less organized international relations. The question of the optimum degree of decentralization then arises.

vii.2. In order to attain the general goals enumerated in ch. VI, national policies of such countries will have to satisfy certain conditions, i.e. a certain unification of their economic policy is required. In the terminology introduced before this means that they should adapt their use of supporting and conflicting instruments to the international requirements. Perhaps the most important condition is that they should maintain *monetary equilibrium at a high level of employment.*

vii.3. There are two main groups of instruments for this policy and a number of subsidiary ones. The first main group is that of *financial policy*, consisting of public expenditure policy and tax policy. By an appropriate manipulation of these instruments total internal demand will be kept at the desired level and its composition may be made optimal.

vii.4. The second group of instruments is that of *wages or exchange rates*. Either of them may be used to adjust the general price level of the country to its competitive strength and hence to regulate foreign demand.

vii.5. Necessity of understanding in business circles for measures just discussed.

vii.6. Desirability of a centralized use of the instruments of economic policy discussed. In view of the strong resistance to integration in this field the centralization might be confined to central decisions about the 'inflationary' or 'deflationary gap' in the public sector and the general price level of each country.

vii.7. These two main groups of instruments may have to be supplemented by others, in order to make minor adjustments.

Temporary subsidies, specific taxes or even *temporary import duties* may be necessary to support industries or regions whose competitive force falls short of the requirements. In the case of sudden disturbances of equilibrium or of particular industries, *quantitative* regulations may be needed. None of these policies should in the long run hamper the correct use of the productive resources from the international point of view.

CHAPTER VIII. *The Integration of Current Transactions*

VIII.I. This chapter deals with the *non-monetary* instruments of economic policy which are relevant in particular for the current items on the balance of payments: trade and current transactions in services. It discusses the policies needed to integrate these transactions between nations. The instruments are in particular *quantitative restrictions* and *import duties*, the primary subjects of (negative) integration.

VIII.2. Certain preliminary conditions have to be fulfilled: the *full use of productive resources* should be warranted by an appropriate national policy. As a supplement to these internal policies and a further condition to economic stability, international co-operation in order to stabilize raw material prices is advocated. This stabilization may be obtained by a system of commodity agreements or by the introduction of a *'raw material standard'*.

VIII.3. Since the optimum division of labour is obtained mostly by free trade, *abolition of quantitative restrictions and of import duties* is advocated. Because of inevitable losses of transition a *gradual* abolition will be optimal.

VIII.4. Certain well-known exceptions (agriculture, infant industries) may be admitted. *Subsidies preferable*, however, in so far as organizational difficulties are not too large.

VIII.5. Abolition of duties will require adjustments in the *rates of exchange*.

VIII.6. Abolition or reduction of quantitative restrictions and import duties may be effectuated for the economy as a whole or for one sector after the other *(partial integration)*; in the latter case there are dangers, however, of disequilibria and tensions.

VIII.7. Alongside negative integration there is a need for *positive integration:* the need for the equalization of certain duties and taxes and the need for a deliberate organization of the optimum division of labour. The latter need not be a task of public authorities.

VIII.8. Attempts to estimate the extent of the consequences of integration.

CHAPTER IX. *Monetary Integration*

IX.1. This chapter deals with the *monetary* instruments, i.e. with the techniques of international payments and their integration. The simplest theoretical solution would be the introduction of a *world currency*, but political unity would be its prerequisite. It is probable, moreover, that capital flight from war-threatened countries would disturb such a monetary sytem. Impossibility to liberalize capital transactions completely.

IX.2. A system of national currencies almost equivalent to a world currency. *Flexible exchange rates*, as advocated before World War II, seemed useful during the confusion of the Great Depression, but imply more arbitrariness than seems desirable. Something more similar to the gold standard, with a *minimum of autonomous changes*, seems more attractive.

IX.3. The changes should be under international control, but in practice this is difficult. Their frequency will be reduced if equilibrium in the balances of payments is preserved as much as possible. National *reserves* and an international equalization fund, such as the I.M.F., will be helpful to overcome short-term disequilibria. In order to warrant long-term equilibrium national policies should be directed towards *monetary equilibrium* and a *competitive price and wage level*.

IX.4. Apart from these policies *capital movements* may help to maintain equilibrium. Short-term capital movements are not always helpful ('hot money'), and long-term movements might be used for this purpose to a greater extent, as in the case of dollar scarcity and of the Italian balance of payments. The distribution of a country's assets and liabilities over the various degrees of liquidity should be such as not to disturb equilibrium.

IX.5. The Second World War caused heavy disturbances in financial equilibria that have only partly been overcome; the question of the *sterling balances* being the most important example. In large parts of the world current items of the balances of payments were thrown out of equilibrium too, necessitating numerous restrictions in trade and payments. Early attempts at restoring convertibility of sterling by decree were not successful.

IX.6. In 1950 mutual convertibility between European currencies was introduced by the establishment of the *European Payments Union*, which was prolonged in 1952 and 1954. The system was not completely self-contained, however. Nevertheless the Western European situation as a whole was very near to equilibrium in 1954. Dollar convertibility for a number of European countries would seem possible; there remains the question of some of the weaker European countries as well as of many underdeveloped countries. A complete solution of the world's payments problems would have to be based on (a) a programme of capital transfers, (b) further reductions in tariffs of the strong countries, (c) more orthodox financial policies in a number of weaker countries.

CHAPTER X. *The Integration of Development*

x.1. So far international economic policy has been discussed on the basis of a given distribution of resources over nations. As was discussed already in ch. I this distribution, however, is far from satisfactory. Its extreme unevenness may be source of important future tensions: the *divergency of living standards* threatens political unity.

x.2. *Factor price equalization* only works to a limited extent as long as factors are not permitted to move. Necessity for factors to move, i.e. of capital transfers and population transfers. Necessity also, to integrate the process of growth. Impossibility to neglect *population problem*.

x.3. Raising the standards of life of the poorer countries by decree is an economic impossibility: prescription of higher wages e.g. will lead to more unemployment. Rise in production needed, requiring a simultaneous increase in *capital* and training and spread of *technical knowledge*. Nature of investments needed first. Impossibility to increase capital formation inside the countries concerned to as sufficient degree.

x.4. Order of magnitude of capital transfers needed in order to stop divergency of living standards. Order of magnitude of present capital transfers. Impossibility to attract private capital from abroad. Desirability of an *'international budget'*. Necessity of an efficient use of capitals involved.

CHAPTER XI. *The Agencies of International Economic Co-operation*

xi.1. In the preceding chapters a system of international economic policy and the corresponding tasks in various fields were described. We will now discuss what agencies will have to be charged with these tasks. To what extent will the existing national agencies be able to perform them, to what extent will they have to be switched over to existing or new international agencies? The problem is intimately connected with the problem of *political integration*. The common economic policy itself may be less or more interventionist which should also depend on circumstances. As long as the preparedness to co-operate falls short of the degree of co-operation needed, less effective methods will have to be followed. Tasks of local or national interest only should of course be left to local or national organs. It is primarily where one government may adversely or favourably affect the interests of other nations that a central agency will be needed. With the former, the central agency will be a supervising rather than an active agency. Agencies to be arranged according to instruments of economic policy. General and partial instruments and agencies. From our survey it has become clear that general agencies will be needed for six groups of tasks, to be discussed in succession. In principle all these tasks should be performed on a world basis. With the unhappy controversy between the Communist and the Non-Communist countries incomplete provisions may be unavoidable. Moreover, regional integration may be useful as an example or because of differences in technical level. In principle, agencies have been created by the United Nations for each of the six main tasks indicated, but various difficulties have been encountered.

XI.2. The *supervision and reduction of trade restrictions* should have been the task of I.T.O., which has not, however, come into existence. Although the tasks with regard to trade restrictions have been taken over by the G.A.T.T., the main difficulties are (i) the unwillingness of many countries to go faster into the direction of free trade, and (ii) the extremely complicated technique adopted to negotiate reductions in tariffs. Although considerable advance has been made on a European basis, within O.E.E.C., to reduce quantitative restrictions, the gains are not permanent. The difficulties encountered point to the necessity of financial integration.

XI.3. The *regulation of raw material markets* is in principle entrusted to the F.A.O. and to the Raw Materials Conference, created after the Korean crisis. A considerable degree of success has been obtained with the Wheat Agreement which succeeded in keeping prices of wheat at a stable and moderate level since 1949. Activities with regard to raw materials have not been too promising. Various U.N. experts' reports stress the importance that more be done in this field. It is less the machinery that is lacking than the preparedness of governments to commit themselves. Possibly the 'Raw Material Standard' might be a simpler solution.

XI.4. The *supervision of the convertibility of currencies* and a number of related tasks are the tasks of the International Monetary Fund, which represents an international reserve bank though with only limited competence and very limited means. Among the international institutions created by the United Nations the Fund is no doubt the best prepared and the best equipped, qualitatively speaking. The possibilities for the Fund are, however, far too restricted: as the experts just quoted emphasize, a reserve of about $ 3 milliards in hard currency is much too little when moderate cyclic fluctuations may easily create a temporary need for about $ 10 milliards. This is why these experts rightly propose an increase in the quota and a more liberal use of the means. By E.P.U. and the Sterling Area arrangements convertibility within restricted non-dollar areas was established. If sterling and some continental currencies are made convertible, some assistance to the remaining inconvertible currencies will be needed.

XI.5. The *supervision of monetary equilibrium* is less clearly the task of an existing agency. Together with other elements of *employment policy*, monetary equilibrium of the member countries is now annually being discussed in the Economic and Social Council of the U.N., on the basis of extensive reports asked from the governments. Although such a discussion in public may certainly have some positive influence on the governments that may be in default, there is no direct competence of any institute to give directives to the governments concerned. This seems to be too weak a construction. A similar situation prevails at the European level. There have been discussions on the internal and external financial stability of the co-operating countries. In case a country shows either an accumulated deficit or a surplus of a certain size and wishes to restrict its imports it will have to explain its policy to the other members. But also in the O.E.E.C. a firm employment policy is lacking.

XI.6. The most important instrument in influencing both the employment situation and development generally is *public finance*. Desirability of an international agency prescribing the inflationary or deflationary gaps in public finance. Sanctions might be found in restricting credit facilities for the weaker countries and non-participation in the execution of international investment projects for the stronger countries. Importance of a '*common budget*'.

XI.7. The task of *supplying capital for development* pertains to the International Bank, and some partial schemes (Colombo Plan, Technical Assistance, Point Four). Limitations to the Bank's activity have led to the proposal to create a Special U.N. Fund for Economic Development; but more resources than have so far been promised are needed. Importance, also for this purpose, of a *common budget*. The same applies to the European situation, especially in view of the problems of Southern Italy.

An international regulation of migration would seem to be farther ahead than any of the other tasks mentioned. The problem cannot be separated from the population problem, an undogmatic approach to which is needed.

xi.8. Summary of findings; centres of activity from which fresh initiatives may emanate; the desirability of financial integration the most important single conclusion reached.

TABLES

I   Population, Area per Head and Capital per Head for some Countries.

II Real Income per 2500 Hours of Work, in I.U., 1925/29.

III Income per Head in $, 1949.

IV Average Import Duties in a Number of Countries 1913, 1925 and 1953.

V   Some Data about the National Wealth and Foreign Investments of Four Countries.

VI Example of Balance of Payments: United States, 1953.

VII Simplified Scheme of Payments Regulations of Sterling Area.

VIII Trade and Its Presumable Changes as a Consequence of a Customs Union between the Countries of the Coal and Steel Community.

DIAGRAMS

1 Composition of World Trade (T) in and World Production (P) of the Principal Basic Products (1936/37).

2 National Income and Imports of a Number of Countries, 1930.

3 Composition of a Network of Flows from Elementary Flows.

4 An example of Classical Discount Policy.

MAP

The Influence of Distance on the Composition of Imports.

FIRST PART

THE ESSENCE OF INTERNATIONAL ECONOMIC
RELATIONS BETWEEN AUTONOMOUS NATIONS

CHAPTER I

INTRODUCTION

THE HETEROGENEITY OF WORLD ECONOMY

1.1. This book is an attempt to clarify the main problems of international economics and of international economic policy for those who are not economists by profession, but take an interest in these problems. Not being written for specialists, it tries to give a simple approach to the problems without neglecting, however, some of the complications that have proved to be of importance to practical problems of international economic co-operation. For the same reason it also deals with some common misunderstandings about the subject.

The *desirability of international co-operation* is taken as the starting point of this book. International co-operation is conceivable in nearly every field of human activity. Economic co-operation is only one of its aspects. It has sometimes been considered as the basic aspect, particularly by those who consider economic relations generally to be basic to human relations. The big and dramatic interruptions of international co-operation which we call wars have, in this same train of thought, been explained by economic causes. The occurrence of the Second World War has shown the limits of this philosophy only too clearly. Certainly autonomous factors of another kind are at work in the causation of war and hence other forms of co-operation than purely economic co-operation will be very important in the struggle for peace. Nevertheless economic factors remain of importance too, by the simple fact that economic activity must necessarily, in a poor world, take up a large part of total human life. International economic co-operation therefore still constitutes an essential part of international co-operation generally. This text deals with its nature and problems. In Part I we will consider the essence of international relations in the economic field; Part II is devoted to the question in what respect these relations should be the subject of deliberate regulation; in a modern terminology it deals with international economic *integration* where this term is taken to express the optimum of international economic co-operation.

1.2. International economic relations are a subject by itself because of the fact that *world economy is not homogeneous*. On the contrary, the world is divided in sixty national economies showing wide differences in their more relevant features and being even themselves often not very homogeneous. In several respects these national economies are almost independent from each other; in other respects, however, they are intimately connected, as will be clear from our further analysis.

In order to get a first rough picture of the heterogeneity of world economy we may describe the national economies by taking their *population* and their *wealth*. It is well known that populations show large differences in quantity as well as in quality. The wealth of any nation consists of two components: (i) its *natural wealth*, such as land for agricultural purposes, minerals, natural means of communication, geographic position and climate, and (ii) the *capital goods* it owns, i.e. the goods partly produced by human labour which are used for further production or consumption: buildings, roads, harbours, machinery, raw material stocks, stocks of consumer goods. Table I gives some figures about the population and the wealth per head of some national economies, among which the most important.

TABLE I

POPULATION, AREA PER HEAD AND CAPITAL PER HEAD
FOR SOME COUNTRIES

Countries	Population on 31 Dec. 1938 in millions	Area in sq. kil. per 1000 inhabitants[1]	Capital in I.U.[2] per head of the working populations[3]
U.S.A.	131	61	4360
Canada	11	870	4240
Gr. Britain and N. Ireland	48	5.1	5000
France	42	13.1	2740
Netherlands	9	4.0	2910
Germany and Austria	76	7.5	2670
Italy	44	7.3	1460
Poland	35	11.3	1200
Australia	7	1130	4400
Russia	170	124	1130
Japan	73	5.5	1350
India and Pakistan	395	12.8	580
China	500	133	180

Apart from differences in physical wealth there are differences in *abilities* of the population, in *market* and *social organization* and in *social climate* which may account for the differences in output per head. A big and uniform market e.g. enables a population to apply large-scale methods of production which cannot be used in small areas; free competition may be a better stimulus to pro-

[1] Around 1936; Statistisches Jahrbuch für das Deutsche Reich, 1937, p. 7.
[2] Dollars with the purchasing power of 1925–1934.
[3] Colin Clark, The Economics of 1960, p. 80.

duction than rather rigid forms of social organization; countries with good 'industrial relations', i.e. good relations between management and employees, may show better productivity figures, etc. Very little is known yet about the exact influence of each of these factors on the level of productivity; important attempts to determine them have recently been made, but they seem to be inconclusive as yet.

1.3. In view of the big differences in wealth (in land as well as in capital goods) WAGEMANN, the well-known German statistician, has divided the world into four areas. By the area of 'high-capitalism' he means the countries with a dense population and a high degree of capitalization (high figures for capital per head). As the density of the population is the reverse of the quantity of land available per head, it may also be said that these are the areas with relatively little land or 'space' and with relatively much capital. They are chiefly Europe and the United States; also Japan. A second group of countries constitutes the area of 'half-capitalism', they are poor in land *and* in capital; chiefly China and India. A third group consists of the 'new-capitalistic' countries; here there is comparative wealth of capital and land; they are the British 'dominions' and South America. The remaining territory, which in view of its population may be called insignificant and is chiefly formed by large parts of Africa, WAGEMANN called the 'non-capitalistic' area. It is rich in land, but poor in capital.

1.4. In each of the national economies there is a complicated *process of production* going on: goods and services are created with the aid of the three so-called factors of production: labour, nature or land and capital. These three

32

factors are the same elements which we have already discussed. Labour is supplied by the population and the natural forces are especially those of the soil. As is well known, very different goods and services are being produced: agricultural products such as wheat, rice, potatoes, cotton, butter, etc., mineral raw materials, such as coal, oil and iron; finished products such as clothing, houses and transport equipment, and services, such as the traffic of goods, the distribution of consumer goods, the cinema or ladies hairdressing; and an enormous number of semi-finished intermediary products. If we want to get an idea of the total quantity of goods produced by a country, we may calculate the total net value produced, or *national product*. In order to yield comparable figures, the value of each product has to be calculated by applying the same prices in all countries, e.g. the price a commodity had, in a certain period, in the United States. We sometimes call such figures 'real' values, as against the 'nominal' figures, where in each country current prices are applied.

COLIN CLARK, the well-known British statistician, who has made many investigations in this field, has expressed the production of all countries in the amount of dollars for which these goods could be bought in the United States on an average during the period 1925–1934, i.e. a period with five prosperous years and five years of depression[1]. The quantity of goods worth one dollar in that period he calls an International Unit (I.U.). When calculating the net value of production we have — apart from some complications which will not interest the layman — to deduct the value of goods absorbed by the production process, such as imported raw materials, worn-out parts of machines, etc. The result of our calculation is called the real net

[1] Colin Clark, The Economics of 1960, London 1942.

geographical product (in 1925/34 dollars) or real income from home production. (Of course the use of other units than the I.U. would also be permitted.) Income from home production is, for all countries, by far the largest part of national income, which includes also income from other sources, such as foreign investment. Real income from home production calculated per head appears to diverge largely for different countries. COLIN CLARK states that calculated per head of the population and assuming everyone is working 2500 hours per year income, in I.U., was in 1925/29:

TABLE II

REAL INCOME PER 2500 HOURS OF WORK,
IN I.U. 1925/29

United States	590
Canada	550
United Kingdom	502
Netherlands	357
Germany and Austria	292
Poland	117
Russia	95
India (incl. Pakistan, Birma and Ceylon)	64
China (incl. Korea and Formosa)	44

Currently figures are being calculated by the United Nations which in various respects are more accurate but in others less appropriate for our purpose, although also illustrative of the lack of homogeneity in world economy. Such figures are e.g. the figures of national income per head expressed in one currency, namely dollars. They are not so well comparable since they disregard price differences; but the differences in prices are much less than

34

those in incomes and therefore they still have some illustrative power. The most recent of these figures are given here:

TABLE III

INCOME PER HEAD IN $, 1949

United States	1453	Israel	389
Canada	870	Czechoslovakia	371
Sweden	780	Western Germany	320
United Kingdom	773	U.S.S.R.	308
Norway	587	Italy	235
Belgium	582	Egypt	100
Netherlands	502	India (1948/49)	57
France	482	China	27

Source: Nat. and per Capita Incomes of Seventy Countries-1949, U.N. (Stat. Papers, Series E no 1, New York 1950).

Of these figures those for Western Germany were in rapid development and may therefore be less comparable. It appears from this table, as it did from table II, that the most important underdeveloped countries among the larger nations are China and India.

1.5. It has been observed already that there are various *reasons* for these differences. One, as we saw, is the difference in *capital per head and land per head* available for production. The low figure for China, e.g., is partly connected with the fact that in that country only about 4 acres (1.6 hectare) is available per farmer, whereas 13 acres is the most economic size. This makes it compulsory to follow methods of production leading to a much lower return than would otherwise have been obtained. Moreover the quantity of capital goods, i.e. agricultural machinery, cattle etc. per head is very low; all in all, the Chinese farmer produces only 1/14 of what his American colleague produces.

As already noted, the extent of the quantitative influence of the various factors is not yet known quite exactly. Some investigations suggest that the influence of capital per head is rather important; an increase by 1 per cent of capital per head may yield an increase in product per head by 1/4 or 1/3 per cent (P. DOUGLAS).

It has become customary, in recent years, to use the concept of the 'capital coefficient', i.e. the ratio between total capital of a country and its total income, or, as the case may be, between an increase in capital and the accompanying increase in income. The former ratio might be called the average capital coefficient; the latter the marginal capital coefficient. Since the increase in capital over a certain period represents the country's net investments, the marginal capital coefficient may also be defined as the ratio of net investment to the increase in income. The numerical values of capital coefficients are only known very crudely and are between 3 and 6. It is interesting to note that they do not show, in countries for which older statistics are available, very much change over the last century. It should be kept in mind that the increase in income need not necessarily be caused by an increase in capital only.

It is also obvious that, within certain boundaries at least, an increase in land available per head will also tend to increase production per head. Formulated in another way, population density will affect productivity, and hence welfare, in an inverse way. There is some difference of opinion about this point; it is sometimes maintained that the relation is more complicated and that up to certain densities an increase in population density will increase productivity; since in the end the opposite tendency will prevail, there will be at least one point in which productivity is a maximum. This point of density is called the optimum density or *optimum population* point. The reason why up to that point an increase in density may be favourable to productivity may be that certain activities can be organized more efficiently. This will be true for industries where mass production is much more productive than small-scale production; it will also be true e.g. for the transportation of commodities. Whether these tendencies are important enough to counteract the opposite tendencies in the other industries has so far hardly been investigated. The impression of the present author, obtained from statistical analysis, is that the optimum is very near to the lowest densities registered for countries as a whole and that therefore by far the larger part of world population is living in countries with more than an optimum population.

Investigations as to the influence of another important factor, the *innate skill* of the population, are contradictory. In a number of cases it is reported that rather primitive populations can easily be trained in modern industrial activities. On the other hand it is only too well known that the business spirit of several oriental populations is very little developed, leading to a pronounced indifference towards increasing their standards of life as soon as some customary level has been reached. One should be careful, however, not to confuse the consequences of a lack of capital or land with those of the innate personal abilities of the population. The apparent 'backward' methods of the Chinese farmer, for example, are to a great extent a result of that lack of equipment; in the given circumstances they still yield the best return.

Recently some attempts have been made to measure the

influence of a third factor, *the extent and organization of the market*. The impression is that the stimulus given by free competition is very powerful and has been underestimated by European politicians. A fourth factor, the *'social climate'* or the *'industrial relations'*, the human relations between management and workers, is also of considerable importance.

1.6. The total product of a country is finally spread over the various *groups of the population* by means of a process of exchange. The proportions going to labour, capital and land are not always known very exactly, although an increasing number of investigations has recently been published. As far as our information goes there is the curious tendency for these proportions to be about the same under very different conditions. This is true in particular e.g. for the distribution of income in the United Kingdom and the United States during the last half of the nineteenth and the first quarter of the twentieth century. But within certain limits it is equally true for a number of other countries and for recent years, although there is a tendency for labour income to rise in comparison to the other incomes. The ratios observed for the period just stated were 70 per cent for labour, 20–25 per cent for capital and 5–10 per cent for land owners. The relative constancy of these figures implies that in periods or countries where one of the factores is scarce its renumeration per unit is very high in comparison to other periods or countries. Capital income per unit of capital was much higher in 1850 in the United States than in 1910 or 1940; labour income per hour of work was very much lower in 1850 than it is nowadays. Labour income is also much lower in China than in France; and much lower in France than in the

United States, according to the different relative scarcities of labour in these countries.

1.7. Between these national economic units of so widely diverging a character there are *various forms of economic intercourse*. They may, for the sake of convenience, be roughly subdivided in:

(1) Exchange of products against products, i.e. current trade in commodities or goods or services;

(2) Transfer of factors of production, i.e. of

    (a) persons or migration;
    (b) land, which occurs as a consequence of changes in territory; and
    (c) capital, known as capital exports and imports.

From the economic point of view (b) is not a common form of intercourse, but a consequence of political events. If it occurs, it is accompanied by transfers of type (2a) and (2c). In the interwar period (2a) did not take place to any appreciable extent either, contrary to what happened in earlier periods. By far the most important forms of intercourse are those under (1) and (2c). In the following chapters we will consider more closely each of these forms of intercourse; in addition we shall study their financial aspects.

Chapter II

CURRENT TRANSACTIONS

II.I. When speaking of current transactions between countries we are thinking of *imports* and *exports* of products, i.e. *goods and services*, and not of factors of production. They may be exemplified by the exports from tropical areas of cotton, cane sugar, coffee, cocoa, coprah etc. to the temperate zones and the imports, the other way round, of textiles, machinery, ships or motor cars. From countries with rich ore deposits iron, copper, zinc and many other metals flow in a continuous stream to other regions; agricultural districts will ship their butter, cheese, meat, hides and wool; horticultural areas supplying fruits and vegetables. From these examples the underlying reason for these transactions — to be discussed more fully later — may already be clear. One country is more appropriate, in view of its climate, the special skill of its population or its capital resources, to supply one type of goods, another country is better equipped to supply another kind of goods. There will be all the more reason to convey such goods along vast distances if they are of high value in proportion to their transport costs. Very heavy goods of comparatively little value, such as coal, iron ore or potatoes, will in general not be transported very far; they seldom cross the oceans (cf. diagram I).

Every good has a certain maximum distance — slightly varying according to circumstances — beyond which it will hardly be able to compete. Generally speaking, therefore, large countries have smaller imports and exports in proportion to total production than small countries. This is

COMPOSITION OF WORLD TRADE (T) IN, AND WORLD PRODUCTION (P)
OF THE PRINCIPAL BASIC PRODUCTS (1936/7).

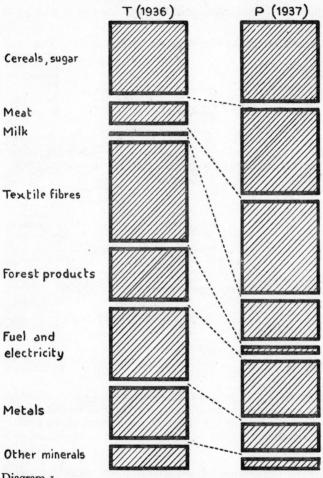

Diagram 1.

Badly transportable goods such as milk play a much slighter part
in international trade than in international production; for easily
transportable and specifically highly valuable goods, such as
textile fibres, it is just the other way about.

illustrated by diagram 2, giving a survey of international trade compared with the national incomes of the principal countries. In the column of imports one can compare the

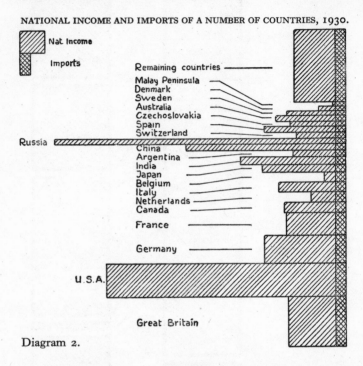

NATIONAL INCOME AND IMPORTS OF A NUMBER OF COUNTRIES, 1930.

Diagram 2.

The parts of the right-hand column show the significance of each of the countries to world trade, the two quadrangles in each horizontal bar show the extent of the imports of the country concerned with respect to the national income of that country.

relative importance of the different countries for world trade, while every horizontal quadrangle gives an idea of the ratio between imports and national income for each country. Although, therefore, a country such as the U.S.A. is of great

42

importance to world trade, yet the imports of that country are only small if compared with its national income.

The influence of distance on the choice of suppliers is illustrated by the map below which will be selfexplanatory.

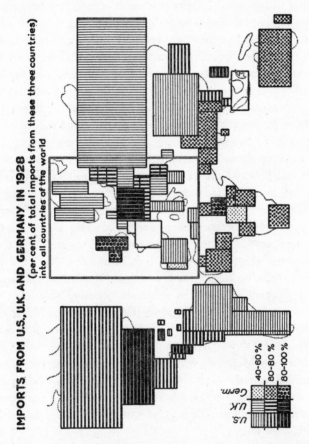

II.2. The flows of current transactions may be represented by the total *money value of these transactions*. Between the

large number of countries in the world there is a network of such flows. They will, as a rule, be *multilateral*, i.e. each country imports from and exports to a large number of other countries. In the short run, there is no necessity for equilibrium between the imports and exports (both taken in the widest sense) of any one country; each country may have an 'overall' deficit or an 'overall' surplus. A deficit will have to be paid for from the reserves of the country or from credits granted by other countries. Even if there is equilibrium in transactions as a whole, there is no necessity for an equilibrium between imports from and exports to any other country separately; there need not be '*bilateral* equilibrium'.

In order somewhat better to understand the nature of a network of flows we may imagine how such a network could be built up from a number of elements. As elements we may use flows of different length. The shortest flow conceivable are those between two countries only, i.e. starting in one country A and finishing in another country B. There may be flows of increasing length, passing along intermediate stations; the *length* may be indicated by the number of countries they connect, minus one. In figure 3, flow 2, running from A to B and from B to C, would have a length 2. There are, in principle, flows of any length. We may, in addition, introduce the concepts of *closed* or *circular flows* or *circuits* (flow 3) and *open flows* (flow 4). With closed flows the starting country and the finishing country are identical; with open flows they are not. The simplest type of a closed flow is one of length 2, ending in the same country in which it starts and having only one intermediary station (flow 5); it will also be called *bilateral equilibrium flow*.

All these elementary flows may be of different *strength* or *width* (i.e. in our case, money value).

COMPOSITION OF A NETWORK OF FLOWS FROM ELEMENTARY FLOWS.

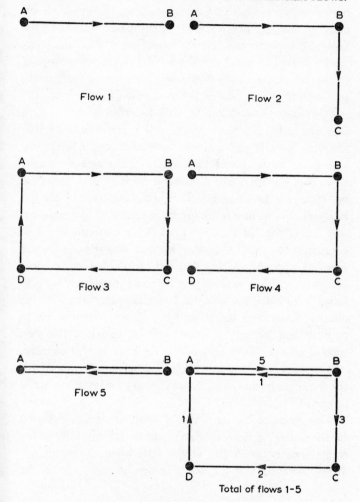

Figures indicate intensities of flows

Diagram 3

1 : Flow of length 1 ; 2 : flow of length 2 ; 3 : closed or circular flow of length 4 ; 4 : open flow of length 3 ; 5 : closed flow of length 2 (bilateral equilibrium flow).

In order that a network of flows be a complete *equilibrium network*, i.e. that for each country total imports are equal to total exports, it should be composed only of closed flows. A network may be an *incomplete* equilibrium network, if equilibrium exists only for a certain group of countries; then open flows would also be permitted, provided they start and end outside the group.

Whereas a network can be built up from its elements in one way only, the decomposition of a given network into simpler flows is not an easy operation and not an unambiguous one either. Different alternative sets of circular flows may lead to one and the same network and hence the network may be decomposed in different ways. Only the bilateral equilibrium flows can be determined in a univocal way by taking, of the two total flows between any two countries, the smallest of the two and adding one of equal size but opposite to that smallest. After deducting these bilateral equilibrium flows one obtains the bilateral surplus flows, which are the sum total of the open flows and the circular flows with length above 2. If a country is not in equilibrium, its 'net position' will be equal to the sum total of all open flows which start or finish in that country.

The concepts just introduced are of some importance for the organization of payments between a set of countries (cf. ch. IV).

The geographical structure of world trade is illustrated by the following figures[2] which indicate the intensity of the total flows between any of the four areas distinguished. It will be clear that the net positions of each area can be

[1] Excl. of U.S.S.R.

[2] Taken from Dr F. Hartog, 'Het probleem van de optimale protectie-eenheid', Econ.-Stat. Ber. 39 (1954) p. 28 and p. 46 (Source: Monthly Bull. of Statistics, U.N.).

Importers:	Exporters				
	Europe[1]	North America	Latin America	Other Areas	Total
Europe[1]	13.1	4.4	1.6	6.8	25.9
North America	2.3	5.2	3.8	1.5	12.8
Latin America	1.7	3.6	0.6	0.3	6.2
Other areas	6.7	1.7	0.8	2.1	11.3
Total	23.8	14.9	6.8	10.7	56.2

found by comparing their import total (last line) and their export total (last column). The bilateral equilibrium components are 2.3 between Europe and North America, 1.6 between Europe and Latin America, 3.6 between North America and Latin America, etc. Trade between Europe and North America and trade within these areas, together cover half of the world trade.

11.3. As to the organization of trade three states may be distinguished: it may be (i) completely *free*, i.e. not subject to any permission or payment, or it may be (ii) *hampered* by one or more of such impediments, in a more or less arbitrary way, or finally it may be (iii) *controlled*, i.e. completely subjected to permissions. The first state has hardly ever existed in pure form, but was approached during the last century and a half by a number of countries following a free-trade policy. In scientific discussions it plays an important role, to be examined below. The state of complete control, meaning that all transactions are subject to government decisions, is to be found in the countries of the communist block and is approached by other countries in war time. That control will, under those circumstances, be directed on the basis of some general program or plan derived from the aims of economic policy in general. The intermediate form of 'hampered' trade is the one existing in most non-communist countries at present; it is applied somewhat more incidentally and as a corrective on free trade. The very fact that they are only applied incidentally sometimes makes them more arbitrary or seem to be so than in the case of complete control. In both cases the foreign tradesman feels that he lacks any certainty or influence as to vital aspects of his existence.

The 'permissions' just mentioned may be based either on a system of *quantitative restrictions* or *quotas* or on a system of *currency restrictions;* the payments to be made are usually *import duties*, and incidentally other payments. Quantitative restrictions are imposed if only a certain quantity and no more of a certain commodity is admitted per year; currency restrictions if only a certain amount of certain types of foreign currency (e.g. dollars) is made available. To the trader who does not get his permission to import it hardly matters on what ground: both restrictions restrict trade. Quantitative restrictions are also sometimes applied to exports; evidently this happens in time of scarcity of goods, whereas the tendency to restrict imports prevails in time of scarcity of foreign currency or severe competition. Payments sometimes may take the form of extra payments to obtain foreign currency, meaning that a concealed devaluation is applied; there may also some-times be export duties; or there may be 'compensatory duties' to be paid with imports, if the commodity considered is taxed inside the country by an excise or a custom. In the latter case the intention of the compensatory duty is the equal treatment of foreign and home producers.

Whereas quantitative restrictions have been severe during the Great Depression and shortly after World War II, they are now, at least between the member countries of

TABLE IV

AVERAGE IMPORT DUTIES IN A NUMBER OF COUNTRIES, 1913, 1925[1] AND 1953[2], EXPRESSED IN PER CENT OF THE PRICES OF THE COMMODITIES

	All articles			Industrial prod.		
	1913	*1925*	*1953*[3]	*1913*	*1925*	*1953*
Argentine	26	26	.	28	29	.
Australia	(17)	(25)	.	(16)	(27)	.
Austria	18	12	.	18	16	.
Belgium	6	8	12[4]	9	15	10[4]
Canada	18	16	.	26	23	.
Czechoslovakia	18	19	.	18	27	.
Denmark	9	6	7	14	1	5
France	18	12	21	20	21	17
Germany	(12)	(12)	26[5]	(13)	(20)	15[5]
Great Britain	0	(4)	16	0	(5)	17
Hungary	18	23	.	18	27	.
India	4	14	.	4	16	.
Italy	17	17	.	18	22	.
Netherlands	3	4	12	4	6	10
Poland	.	23	.	.	32	.
Spain	33	44	.	41	41	.
Sweden	16	13	9	20	16	7
Switzerland	7	11	.	9	14	.
United States	33[6]	29	12[7]	44[8]	37	12[7]
Yougoslavia	.	23	.	.	23	.

[1] Taux-Indices des Tarifs, publ. League of Nations, 1927 II 34, p. 16.

[2] Moyenne des tarifs (Tome I, II, III, IV), Brussels 1950, Groupe d'études pour l'Union Douanière Européenne, with correction for tariff changes during the intervening period.

[3] Semi-manufactures and finished products.

[4] Belgium and Luxembourg.

[5] Western Germany.

[6] In 1914: 16

[7] 1951; covers the same articles as the League of Nations figures.

[8] In 1914: 25.

the Organization of European Economic Co-operation (O.E.E.C.), reduced to a percentage of total trade lying below 10 per cent, with the exception of French imports. Import duties are still considerable in a number of countries; some data are found in table IV.

There may be blocks of countries with free internal trade and with a common tariff for the outside world or even without any import duties vis-à-vis the outside world. In the first case we speak of a *'customs union'*; the German countries in the latter part of the 19th century and after formed such a union, Belgium and Luxembourg did so after the First World War and since 1948, Belgium, Luxembourg and the Netherlands together form the Benelux union. Trade between the states of the United States of America is also practically free. In the case where no tariffs are applied vis-à-vis the outside world at all we speak of a *'free trade area'*. A customs union may develop into an *economic union* if further steps towards integration are taken. Usually we think of a unification of further taxes and of other aspects of economic policy when speaking of an economic union or of integration. In this text we will define the state of economic integration as the economic policy which shows an *optimum of centralization* (cf. ch. VI). An optimum is not necessarily a maximum; and it depends on many elements of the problem to which extent and in what matters centralization should be aimed at.

11.4. For a correct understanding of the essence of international economic relations it is useful to consider the extreme case, namely the one of *free trade*. In addition it will often be assumed, when investigating the state of free trade, that transportation costs can be neglected. For low-value goods this will not be possible and sometimes therefore we will try to take account of the consequences of transportation costs. Disregarding transportation cost we may state that with free trade, prices of one and the same commodity will be *equal in all countries*. Another characteristic of free trade is that it is *multilateral*: if there are no difficulties in paying for trade transactions it would be pure co-incidence if there were bilateral equilibrium between any two countries (cf. II.2). A country may therefore have, and usually has, deficits with regard to some and surpluses with respect to other countries.

Free trade is not equivalent to what the economist calls free competition. Free or perfect competition has become the scientific term for competition between a large number of competitors, where no single competitor feels able to influence the price level of the market by his acts. Competition is called imperfect if one or more of the competitors are able to influence prices, i.e. if there are monopolistic elements in the market. In international as well as national trade, market imperfections are very common; they may be caused by natural and other monopolistic factors. One of the competitors may have a natural monopoly by finding himself at a short distance from his customers; or his product may have special features which the other producers are unable to supply completely. As a consequence international trade appears, for short-run variations, to show characteristics of rather *imperfect competition*. This is shown by the so-called short-term elasticity of a country's share in world trade with respect to its relative price level. A relative fall in a country's export price level with regard to the export price level of all countries together of, say, one per cent appears to be followed — in the first year or so — by a decrease in that country's share in world exports by no more than 2 per cent. The figure 2 in this case represents the elasticity just mentioned. In the case of perfect competition it should have been, theoretically, infinite. It is often even less than 2. The same applies to the short-term elasticity of imports as a ratio to total home demand with respect to the ratio of import prices to home price level. Both tendencies are connected, it seems, with the difficulty to switch from one supplier to another for the reasons quoted. It is natural and probable that long-term elasticities are higher; and the same applies to the elasticities referring to one single type of goods, especially staples. By short-term reactions in this context we mean reactions taking no more than one or two years. Although, therefore, free trade does not necessarily imply free competition, we will in theoretical analysis often assume them to co-exist.

II.5. International trade may be said to be a consequence of a certain *division of labour*: if everybody produced everything he consumes himself, there would be no trade. The basis of this division of labour is that there are differences in the *relative* efficiency of different industries between countries. In each country there are different factors of production; let us, however, to start with, only speak of labour and later amplify our argument so as to include other productive effort also. With free trade and neglecting transportation costs, there will be one single price on the world market for each product. We choose the units of these products so as to have a price of $ 1 for each commodity. The efficiency of each industry in each country may now be indicated by the quantity produced in one hour. Suppose we have two countries and two industries only; and let their efficiencies be given in the following matrix:

DATA FOR A VERY SIMPLE MODEL OF
INTERNATIONAL TRADE

	Quantity produced by one man-hour:	
	Product 1	Product 2
Country 1	1	0,91
Country 2	0,42	0,50

In these circumstances it will be clear that country 1 will
do wisely to produce only product 1 and country 2 only
product 2. A man-hour used by country 1 in industry 2
would yield only $ 0.91 of worth, whereas one man-hour
in industry 1 yields $ 1.—. If country 1 wants to consume
product 2 it can obtain one unit of it by producing good
1 and exporting it, while buying good 2 for the proceeds.
For country 2 a man-hour used in industry 2 will yield
$ 0,50 of worth and by exchanging it on the world market,
½ unit of 1 may be obtained which is more than would be
got by producing good 1 directly. What matters is that
relative efficiencies are decisive, not absolute. Country 1 is
more efficient, in absolute terms, than country 2 in producing
good 2; but nevertheless it should not produce good 2. The
above reasoning will have made this clear. In addition it
could be observed that country 1, although producing more
units of 2 per man-hour than country 2, does not produce it
more cheaply. For wages will be much higher in country
1 than in country 2. They will be, if there is perfect
competition between employers, almost $ 1.— per hour in
country 1 and almost $ 0.50 in country 2. Our little model
could be extended to the cases of more industries, more
countries and more factors of production without changing
the basic conclusions on what products will be exported
and what the level of wages (and other incomes) will be.

It illustrates what is called the *'theory of comparative cost'* (cf. also appendix 1).

Similar, but somewhat more complicated statements may be made on the 'division of labour' between a larger number of countries, or a larger number of products, or a larger number of factors of production. With more factors of production the tendency will be to produce as high a total value of production as possible with the help of all factors available. It will be possible to use all units of all factors (say labour, land and capital) only if either (i) the proportion in which these factors are needed are the same for all products and for the country as a whole, or (ii) when this is not so, there is a sufficient 'spread' in these proportions for the various goods. The meaning of this latter condition may be clarified with a simple example of two factors only: labour and land. If a country has 100 units of labour for every unit of land and products exist which, respectively, require 50 and 150 units of labour in combination with one unit of land, it will be possible for the country, by producing equal quantities of both products, to use both factors fully. If, however, only products are known for which the proportions are 50:1 and 75:1 the country concerned will not be able to use all its labour. We shall come back to this problem later; it will not present itself if, in the process of production, there is an unlimited possibility to replace one factor by the other.

11.6. We are now on our way to the *fundamental thesis of the doctrine of free trade* which a long time determined discussions on trade policy and in a way still does. It says that *under certain conditions free trade leads to maximum welfare*. The conditions are just as important as the thesis itself. The most important ones will be dealt with here:

(1) All productive resources are supposed to be used in production, i.e. there are *no idle resources* (unemployed workers or idle capacity);

(2) Prices of products are equal to their *marginal costs*, i.e. to the cost of producing the last unit;

(3) The temporary consequences of adaptations of productive resources to changes in demand are neglected;

(4) Welfare is measured by the *total value of production, at free-trade prices*. This method of measuring welfare is only one of several; one might conceive of the total value of *expenditure* (for consumption and investment) at free-trade prices. It is also significant to note that welfare is assumed to be independent of the distribution of production over individuals or groups of the population.

Under the conditions summed up it is easy to prove the thesis. A system of free trade implies that every country is using its productive resources in the most efficient way, as was illustrated by our little model. Alternative uses would be those resulting from some form of protection or from another method of pricing. They would always result in using the resources in a less efficient way; in our example e.g. in the use of labour in industry 2 by country 1, or in the use of labour in industry 1 by country 2. The interesting point to note is that not only total welfare would decline, but also the welfare of any one country involved. If protection therefore is an advantage for some groups of the population, it must at the same time be a disadvantage for other groups of the same population. This latter part of the proposition only applies, however, as long as we measure welfare by the value of production at free-trade prices. If we measured it by the value of expenditure at free-trade prices, it would no longer be valid for countries *large enough to be able to influence their terms of trade*, i.e. the ratio of prices at which they import and export. Indeed large countries may, by imposing a tariff, depress demand of some import products and so get them, as a nation, cheaper than without such a tariff. And they might apply tariffs in such a way as to maximize the volume of goods they obtain by production and trade. The tariff which makes this volume a maximum has been called the '*optimum tariff*.' The optimum of course refers to the country concerned. Since the imposition of whatever tariff always decreases the total value of production of the world at large, any advantages obtained by one country would be at the expense of other countries. There may be cases where this might by itself be a positive contribution to welfare, if welfare is to imply certain aspects of *distribution* also. The same advantage to the first country might, however, have been reached in other ways also, namely by producing according to a free-trade régime and by subsidizing that country.

Marginal cost pricing may not be possible in some industries, without subsidizing them. If marginal costs are below average costs, this method of pricing would imply permanent losses to the industry concerned. Marginal costs should be taken to mean long-term marginal costs, however, and then it is doubtful whether there are many industries for which these are lower than average costs. Even if they were, however, certain types of subsidies would be preferable to protection from a purely economic point of view — i.e. disregarding possible difficulties of administrative organization. They would be preferable if they left prices equal to free-competition prices of which it can be proved that they maximize welfare; the use made of productive resources would yield a higher utility.

Full use of resources has also been mentioned as a con-

56

dition for the validity of the free trade doctrine. If they are not fully used, tariffs may contribute to their fuller use and so increase production. For practical political purposes this condition may be interpreted to mean that the full advantages of free trade (through division of labour) can only be reaped if the full use of resources is warranted by an appropriate policy of full employment, or at least of high and stable employment. Such a policy, which may be largely a 'compensatory' financial policy, will be discussed in chapter VII.

II.7. The propositions so far discussed all referred to *long-term adaptations;* as was expressed in our condition (3), temporary consequences of adaptations may be neglected if the advantages to be obtained are of a lasting character. In reality they never are; and temporary adaptations do count therefore, especially since they represent disadvantages that have to be suffered before any advantages will be observable. An *optimum policy* leading from a state of protection towards one of free trade will therefore always have to be a policy where such a period of adaptation will have to be taken such as to maximize *net* advantages (discounted over time in some acceptable way). Here, net advantages are the advantages obtained from free trade, minus the disadvantages of adaptation, such as the cost of retraining workers and of extra investments.

Protection may therefore be acceptable for periods of adaptation to new circumstances. It may even be acceptable if it did not exist previously, if import duties are by far the simplest device to temporarily support an industry whose sudden disappearance would be too difficult an occurrence.

The same applies to the use of import duties in order to

support an *'infant industry'*; here one could say that by so doing the efficiency of that industry may be raised and that it therefore represents a case where efficiency is not given beforehand as was the case in our matrix in section II. 5. It remains to be seen, nevertheless, whether the same effect cannot be obtained by subvention instead of protection. The danger of protection lies in its 'invisibility' to the public and to the tax-payer and the tendency to maintain it and so to lack the wholesome forces of competition for less productive units.

II.8. After a *period of isolation* as, for example, created by a war, the liberalization of a country's trade presents a subtle problem. It will have to be solved gradually and with great care in order to prevent the sudden disruption of the many partial equilibria on which a war economy is built, before the conditions to general equilibrium are fulfilled. The conditions of such a general equilibrium will be discussed in chapter IV. Only some examples of the problems involved are mentioned here. Before liberalizing foreign trade in a certain commodity the home market should be more or less in equilibrium, which may be tested by the abolition of rationing, if in existence. It is no use anyhow to liberalize trade if there is still rationing and the controls needed for rationing are even in direct contradiction to free trade. Before any more general liberalization of imports is undertaken it should be ascertained that the general price level inside the country is competitive on the world market: otherwise there is a real danger that imports will grow very fast and outgrow exports.

Liberalization of trade will generally also mean the disruption of bilateral equilibria with individual countries which are likely to exist as a consequence of unequal softness of the currencies in war time. There should be parallelism therefore between steps towards a freer trade and steps towards convertibility of money (cf. ch. VIII and IX).

II.9. In an attempt to restore free trade various alternative methods may be followed, to be discussed in some more detail in chapter VIII. One of the so-called partial forms of integration is the establishment, already mentioned, of a customs union between a limited number of countries. It is an interesting question, whether such a *customs union does or does not represent a useful step towards world free trade.* Whereas it is clear that in the end, if world free trade is to be reached, all countries will have to follow the steps taken by the members of some customs union, doubt may arise as to the contribution to the best division of labour which it implies. Probably it will in fact in some ways improve the division of labour. If shoes can be made more cheaply in Holland and glass in Belgium, elimination of trade impediments between these two countries may contribute to a more rational production pattern. But it may also, by the existence of a tariff at the outside frontier of the union, lead to an erroneous increase say in butter production in Holland, if the cheaper potential supplier would have been Denmark. It very much depends on the data of the actual circumstances whether one or the other aspect is more important. A happy formulation of the two aspects of a partial customs union has been VINER's distinction between the *trade-creating* elements and the *trade-diverting* elements of a union, the two elements just exemplified.

Chapter III

INTERNATIONAL MOVEMENTS OF FACTORS: LAND, LABOUR AND CAPITAL

III.1. As observed in chapter I (cf. 1.7), products may not only be the object of economic intercourse between nations, but also movements of factors, be it to a much lesser degree. They will briefly be discussed in this chapter.

Movements of *land*, in the literal sense of the word, are impossible of course. The transfer of territory from one nation to another may, however, be considered an example. This sometimes has assumed considerable dimensions, as may be exemplified by the cases of Austria, Yougoslavia and Rumania after the First World War, the history of Poland and the Baltic States and the reduction in German territory after the Second World War. The common characteristic of all these examples is their political rather than normal economic nature. Considerable increases in territory of course have also occurred in colonial areas, by means which cannot now be considered to be very different from the ones previously mentioned. The more satisfactory examples of any extent are the examples of the exploration and consequent use of newly discovered empty territories, as was almost the case with the United States. The creation of new land by reclamation presents the most attractive form of occupation where not even the slightest chance of depriving other peoples of their resources is involved, but its extent so far has been very modest only. And in a way we are leaving the concept of movement of factors between nations if we are thinking of these one-sided additions to territory.

It may be stated anyhow that transfer of territory is not now considered a normal element of international economic policy.

III.2. Movements of *labour*, i.e. of population, known as *migration*, have been important above all for certain areas of immigration, where they constituted the larger part of the increase in population during some periods. This was particularly the case with the United States of America between 1850 and 1924, when some 30 millions moved to that country. For the countries from which these emigrants moved the significance of the decrease in population pressure was usually only modest: the largest percentage of a population that ever emigrated in one year having been somewhat above 1 per cent.

After 1924 the extent of international migration has been very much reduced. The reason is obvious: to the mass of the workers in an immigration territory it is a disadvantage if workers from poorer countries come in and increase the supply of labour, the consequence being a *pressure on wages*. This conclusion might be erroneous as far as the United States would in fact have a population below the optimum population (cf. Ch. I). But there are reasons to doubt that proposition. This opposition against immigration constitutes a serious example of a conflict of interests between the workers of a wealthy territory and the rest of the world. In general it may be said to be to the advantage of world production if labour is being transferred from countries where its productivity is low to countries where it is high. This conflict is a tragic one. Its solution is hampered by the fact that the supply of labour in the overpopulated areas in the Far East is so endless that the American worker does not see a solution in the admission of immigrants unless at the same time some prospect existed of limiting the supply of labour. In India the government has recognized officially the importance of *'family planning'* and thus a beginning of understanding for this side of the problem has been shown. It is to be hoped that at a later stage, the less populated areas will be prepared to revise their immigration policy under certain guarantees of a check to population increases.

III.3. In the present circumstances, and in fact already since the middle of the nineteenth century, the most important form of international movements of factors is, from the economic point of view, presented by *capital movements*. It may take the form of loans granted by one country to another, upon which regular amortizations and interest have to be paid, or it may take the form of participations, on which no amortization, but dividends are being paid. Loans may be subdivided into short-term and long-term loans. For the process of production long-term loans and participations are the more important types: they come down, in real terms, to the transfer, from one country to the other, of commodity stocks of either durable or non-durable character. Durable commodities like railway equipment, machinery etc. make it possible to create productive enterprises and non-durable supplies to put them into operation. Once they operate they will have to be able to pay their workers from the proceeds of their production; the non-durable supplies are necessary to bridge the gap between the moment when operation starts and the moment when sales are at their normal level. The annual payments of interest and amortization or of dividends represent an annual 'mortgage' of part of the increased production which in the case of a productive investment can be

TABLE V

SOME DATA ABOUT THE NATIONAL WEALTH AND FOREIGN INVESTMENTS OF FOUR COUNTRIES
(000,000,000's omitted)

Country	Year	Currency	National Wealth	Foreign Investments	Further data about the figures in column 5
1	2	3	4	5	6
France	1913	Frs	300	45	Russia 11.3; rest of Europe 16.2; Fr.[1] col. 4.0; remainder 13.5
Germ.	1913	Marks	350	23.5	Austria-Hungary 3.0; rest of Europe 9.5; America 7.5; remainder 3.5
Gr. B.	1914	£	16	3.76	Empire 1.78; U.S.A. 0.76; So. and Cent. Am. incl. Mexico 0.76; remainder 0.46
	1929	£		3.7^2	
	1935	£	21.5	3.8^2	
	1938	£		4.0^2	
U.S.A.	1914	$	107	1.9^2	
	1930	$		15.2^3	Europe 4.9; Asia 1.0; Canada 3.9; Cent. and So. Am. 5.2
	1938	$	220	11.8	
				11.1^2	Canada 3.7; So. Am. 2.5; Europe 2.3; Foreign property in U.S.A. 7.9
	1943	$		13.3	Canada 4.4; Gr. Britain 1.0; other British countries 0.4; Cent. and So. Am. 3.3; Germany 1.3; Italy 0.3 Foreign property in U.S.A. 13.15

[1] Germ. = Germany, Fr. = France, Gr. B. = Great Britain; U.S.A. = United States.

[2] Long term investments only.

[3] Only private-long term investments. In addition, a balance of short-term investments of -1.1 and loans by the government to foreign governments (war loans) 7.7.

actually borne. Usually the lending area will be one of the highly developed and the borrowing area one of the less developed countries. Capital is flowing, in such a case, from countries where it is less productive to countries where it is more productive. These movements of capital contribute, in this way, to a decrease in the inequality of living standards. Whether the process has ever been sufficient to stop the divergency in living standards is doubtful. It is probable that in order to do so these movements would have to be much more important.

Private capital movements, which were an important part of total capital movements before World War I (cf. table V) have diminished because of increasing political uncertainty about the possibilities to receive dividends or interest and amortization. In the colonial era there was, for a number of countries at least, practical certainty about these transfers, whereas in recent periods the tendency to take autonomous decisions increased. These decisions are partly a consequence of decreased monetary stability in the countries concerned and partly of a certain aversion towards private foreign capital.

There is another important aspect to the problem of investment in underdeveloped countries. In a number of cases such investments are not as remunerative as might have been deduced from the scarcity of capital in such countries. In other words: the efficiency of production sometimes is so low as to make such investments hardly attractive. This seems to be due to some extent to the absence of certain general facilities such as energy supply, a good transportation system, reasonable housing conditions and a certain minimum of training of the workers. One may speak, in this connection, of a vicious circle: if for some reason the capital stock per head is low it is difficult to increase it; once the circle were broken, it might be easier to increase capital intensity further. The only way to attain this higher level that seems possible is an international effort, in the *public* sphere, to supply the basic equipment in the sectors just indicated.

III.4. *Short-term capital movements* are not able to contribute in a direct way to the long-term increase of equipment or of commodity stocks of a country. Their action is therefore not to be expected in the commodity sphere but rather in the financial sector. Short-term credits may help to overcome temporary difficulties in the financing of foreign payments and so prevent interruptions in the smooth functioning of the economy. They may promote, by so doing, financial stability, i.e. before all the maintenance of exchange rates during periods of depression and so indirectly contribute to the development process.

Chapter IV

THE MECHANISM OF FINANCIAL TRANSACTIONS

IV.1. The organization of production and consumption in the larger part of most countries is based on a fargoing division of labour, as we have seen, and a complex network of transactions is the consequence, for which payments have to be made. These are made with the aid of various *means of payments*, differing between countries. The only means of payments that is accepted everywhere is *gold;* or, as we express it, gold is 'legal tender' everywhere. Using gold for all payments to be made would, however, be rather expensive in two ways: a considerable value would have to be 'invested' in a country's stock of money in circulation and, in addition, the shipment of gold to other countries requires relatively high costs of transportation, insurance etc. Using paper money is cheaper in both respects and more convenient in many ways. Since paper money has, however, no intrinsic value, it has to derive its value from legal provisions, which link it up with a certain government. and therefore restrict its validity to a certain country. Payments from one country to another therefore require a '*transfer*', i.e. transformation of home money into foreign money. This is effectuated by exchanging the various currencies against each other at a certain market price, called the *exchange rate*.

IV.2. The set of all payments made in a certain period (e.g. a year) between a country and all other countries is called that country's *balance of payments* (cf. table VI). Usually

66

this 'balance' is presented in the form of a table showing on one side all payments made by the country and on the other side all payments received (the debit and the credit side, respectively). It may further be subdivided into the *current items*, which are payments for current transactions in goods and services, and the *capital items*, being payments for property titles in the widest sense, and gold shipments. Among the current items the payments for commodities (imports and exports) together are also called the *balance of trade*, whereas the payments for services, including shipping freights, interest and dividends as payments for 'capital services', tourist receipts, insurance premiums, fees for free professions, etc. are summarized as the *'invisible items'*. As a third category, *unilateral payments* or *donations* may occur in the balance of payments, i.e. payments not offsett by material transactions. Well-known examples of such payments are the foreign aid as received from the United States under the European Recovery Program (Marshall Plan) by European countries and the reparation payments made by Germany after the First World War.

IV.3. Of the various items the gold shipments are often considered to be the *'balancing item'*, necessary to 'pay for the deficit in the other items' (or, as the case may be, receivable because of a surplus in the other items). As a first approximation it may be stated this way, but it should be added that sometimes also short-term capital movements of a certain type perform this function, e.g. short-term credit obtained by some international financial agency or centre. To the extent that a state of disequilibrium influences certain of the items in an automatic way, the gap may partly also be filled by parts of the other items.

If the equilibrating item is included it is obvious that

TABLE VI

EXAMPLE OF BALANCE OF PAYMENTS; UNITED STATES, 1953, IN MILLIARDS OF $

(A equals total of 1–8; B of 9–10; C of 11–19)

	Credits		Debits
A. Goods and Services (net)	4.5		—
1. Merchandise. Exports, f.a.s.	16.4	Imports, f.a.s.	11.9
3. Foreign travel	0.5		0.9
4. Transportation	1.3		1.1
5. Insurance	. .		. .
6. Investment income	1.9		0.4
7. Government, n.i.e.	0.5		2.1
8. Miscellaneous	0.7		0.3
B. Donations (net)	—		6.5
9. Private	—		0.5
10. Official:			
10.1 Military (net)	—		4.3
10.2 Other	—		1.8
Net total (1 through 10.1)			*0.2*
Net total (1 through 10.2)			*2.0*
C. Capital and Monetary Gold (net)	1.7		
11, 15 Long-term liabilities (net)	0.1		
12, 16 Short-term liabilities (net)	1.0		
13, 17 Long-term assets (net)			0.7
14, 18 Short-term assets (net)	0.2		
19 Monetary gold	1.2		
Net errors and omissions and mult. settlements	0.3		

Source: Balance of Payments Yearbook, edited by the International Monetary Fund.

there will always be equilibrium, which for this reason will be called *'formal equilibrium'*. If it is not included, the phrase 'balance of payments' has a different meaning. Thus conceived, it may or may not be in equilibrium. If it is, this balance of payments (second definition) is said to be in '*material equilibrium*'. Under these circumstances the balancing item therefore is equal to zero. In the long run, i.e. as an average over a long period, the situation must be near to material equilibrium: otherwise there would have to be a permanent accumulation of gold somewhere and a permanent drain elsewhere. There may be, however, a modest deviation from material equilibrium for quite some time, e.g. if a country is gradually liquidating a large gold stock, or if a country is producing gold itself. In a way the production of gold could, however, in the latter case, be considered to be a normal economic activity of the country and then the corresponding gold shipments might be classified as exports, which would restore material equilibrium as understood here.

IV.4. The rates of exchange against which foreign money can be obtained are not exactly constant. In this respect there are different systems of organization for foreign payments, some with almost completely stable rates, some with more fluctuating rates. *Stability of exchange rates* is an advantage for economic calculations, but it may be non-compatible with stable prices or with long-term equilibrium in the balance of payments or with other objectives still, which may be considered more desirable. Usually systems are preferred which show very little changes in rates. Incidental revisions may be necessary in the case of 'fundamental disequilibrium', the term used in the Charter of the International Monetary Fund, to indicate situations of a more lasting disequilibrium.

The organization that existed a long time and was known as the '*gold standard*' worked in about the following way.

Under this system there is a fixed price against which the Central Bank buys or sells gold. For each foreign currency, say the dollar, there is one rate of exchange, say in the Netherlands *f* 3,80, which corresponds to this price of gold. It is called the *'parity rate'* or *'parity'*. With the rate at or very near to parity it is more advantageous to pay an American firm by buying dollars than by buying gold and sending this, since transportation of gold is more expensive than a bank transfer. The rate of exchange under the gold standard was not, however, completely stable and responded to fluctuations in demand and supply. If during a certain time unit demand for dollars surpasses their supply, the rate of exchange will rise. Payment in gold may then become relatively more attractive and beyond a certain rate definitely more attractive. This rate is called the *'upper gold point'*. Conversely, if demand is low, a rate may be reached, the *'lower gold point'*, where it becomes more advantageous, for Americans, to ship gold towards the Netherlands. We may summarize this by saying that between the gold points gold shipments are unremunerative. Only a rigorous material equilibrium in the balance of payments will, however, keep the exchange rates within the range of the gold points. *The first line of defence* against disequilibrium thus is a movement of the exchange rate to one of the gold points, and the *second* consists of the automatic shipment of gold. As long as gold is shipped, the rate will remain at one of the gold points. But there is a threat of exhausting the gold stock of the weaker of the two countries if the movement goes on. This may be prevented by further lines of defence. We will speak of (a) 'indirect' and (b) 'direct action'.

IV.5. *Indirect action*, being the *third line of defence*, may be of two types again, to be called automatic and deliberate.

Automatic action occurs as a consequence of the changes in monetary circulation which accompany the gold shipments. If gold is sent by the country considered (Holland) national means of circulation (notes or bank deposits) are offered to the Central Bank for the purchase of gold and so the monetary circulation is drained. The consequences will be, in principle, a reduction in incomes, leading to reduced imports and lower prices. In principle, too, the latter will stimulate exports. It should, however, be observed that this automatism does not work very strongly and quickly. Gold shipments are not usually very important in comparison to total imports and exports and hence their influence on imports and, via prices, on exports will be small. In addition the operation of this mechanism requires time, probably several months. It will be discussed somewhat more extensively in chapter V.

More can be expected, at short notice, from the *deliberate* type of action, which therefore represents the real 'third line' of defence. Its usual form under the gold standard was the raising by the Central Bank, of the *discount rate*, i.e. the interest rate the Bank charges for short credits (on commercial bills). (Some other rates usually were varied at the same time). This rate influences the other, 'free' interest rates in the country and acts in two ways. First, it tends to have similar consequences as just described for automatic action; but these again will be only weak and slow. Secondly, and this is probably the most important consequence, it will attract foreign short-term capital or prevent home short-term capital from being invested elsewhere. To be sure this inflow of short-term capital will only occur if no counteracting 'psychological' factors work, i.e. if a lack of confidence in the future of the currency of the country considered does not offset the purely economic

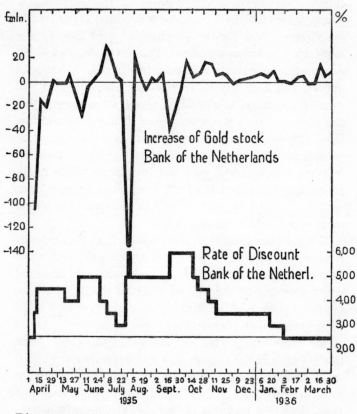

Diagram 4

The rate is raised after every heavy fall in gold stock and lowered
after a recovery in gold holdings.

considerations of yield. The remedy provided by this
inflow can only be a temporary one, since it represents a
shift in the distribution of existing assets, i.e. in the

distribution of 'stocks' and not a continuous flow. It may be an acceptable remedy for a short-term disequilibrium therefore, but it cannot remedy a lasting or 'fundamental' disequilibrium.

The operation and results of 'deliberate indirect action', or, in the usual language, of discount policy, may be well exemplified by the 'defence of the Dutch guilder' during 1935/6 (cf. diagram 4). It will be seen how decreases of the gold stock of the Netherlands were followed by rises in the discount rate which, in their turn, led to a temporary restoration of the reserve. Nevertheless, in September 1936 the decision to devalue had to be taken, together with the only two remaining members of the 'gold block', France and Switzerland.

IV.6. *'Direct action'* may be the only way open and hence the last or *fourth* line of defence, if indirect action appears to be unsuccessful or unpromising. This may be so especially in the case of a 'fundamental disequilibrium', i.e. a disequilibrium in the underlying economic variables, such as the price and cost level of the country concerned.

Such direct action may either consist of a change in the gold price and hence in the parity rates; or it may consist of stopping the sale of gold. In the former case the currency concerned has *devalued;* in the latter case the old parity may be maintained, but the currency will have become *inconvertible:* the parity has then been maintained at the cost of freedom. Both these steps will be a shock to confidence and may therefore disturb the financial structure of the country, at least for a short period. Central Banks and governments will evidently try to avoid them as long as possible; one of the ways to do so being the possession of

73

a large gold reserve. As will be discussed in chapter V, even the largest gold stock will be insufficient, however, if the country is in fundamental disequilibrium.

With a situation of inconvertibility international payments have to be regulated on a basis of *'clearing'*. The simplest form of clearing is possible with respect to the payments for a bilateral equilibrium flow (cf. section II.2): here a direct compensation, without any 'payment' is possible. But also for circular flows of a greater length (cf. II.2) clearing, be it on a multilateral basis, is possible. For open flows the situation is still less easy: here evidently clearing is only possible if the first country in such a flow grants a credit to the last country, which then is able to pay the last but one; this country can pay the last but two, and so on, until the first country obtains payment from the second in the flow. The series of payments just mentioned was made possible, under the European Recovery Program, by a chain of 'drawing rights' of each of the countries concerned on its successor in the chain. No provisions are possible, in a system of clearing, for the remaining 'net positions'.[1]

IV.7. The *'reserve'* or *'cover'* of a currency system represents part of the assets which the Central Bank possesses against the liabilities represented by its note circulation and deposits. The remaining part of the assets usually consists of government bonds of one type or another, which are of no significance, however, as international means of payments. The reserve need not only consist of gold; it consisted, for quite some time, also of silver. And it is conceivable that

[1] Cf. M. H. Ekker, 'Equilibrium of international trade and international monetary compensations', Weltw. Archiv 64 (1950), p. 204.

other commodities be used as well. One special form that has been advocated recently is the system of a *'raw material standard'*, where part of the reserve would consist of warehouse bonds representing the property of certain quantities of raw materials, in a specific composition. The consequences of a raw material standard, i.e. the preparedness of central banks to buy or sell at fixed prices certain 'baskets of raw materials' would be a stabilization of the average price level of the raw materials included. Such a stabilization could contribute to the stabilization of the trade cycle, since that cycle is partly due to variations in the general price level. This is particularly true of the variations in income as calculated by many business firms: changes in inventory prices are often wrongly considered as an element of income. This represents the so-called 'accounting error' to which the business cycle has partly been ascribed by various authors. This error would be considerably reduced by a stabilization of raw material prices.

IV.8. Usually a system of *'flexible exchange rates'* is presented as the opposite of the 'gold standard', though in principle the differences are not large. It operates in a similar way. But quantitatively the differences may be considerable. The main difference of principle is that no automatic shipment of gold is applied: gold is only used by an *Exchange Equalization Fund* run by the government in order to influence exchange rates. If current demand for dollars, e.g., is so much higher than the current supply of dollars as to depreciate the rate of exchange below a certain lower limit, the Fund will supply dollars or gold in order to support the rate. Conversely it may buy dollars or gold during periods of relatively low demand. Usually the lower and the upper limit show a much wider margin — and this is a quantitative difference — than with the gold standard, e.g. 20 per cent as against perhaps 1 per cent.

It should not be forgotten, however, that there is not only one system of flexible rates or only one system of the gold standard. Both occur in a number of alternative versions; and often there has not been any system at all, especially under circumstances where disequilibrium is such that the authorities loose control of the situation. This is particularly so in the case of '*hyperinflation*'. The standard case in modern Western history has been the hyperinflation in Germany in 1922 and 1923. After an initial disequilibrium as a consequence of post-war developments (government deficits financed by money creation) demand for foreign currencies increased more and more because of speculation against the mark and of vanishing confidence in its ultimate recovery. The process became a fall of its exchange rate to one billionth (in the Continental sense of that word, i.e. $1 : 10^{12}$) of the parity rate.

One of the functions of an Exchange Equalization Fund is the prevention and counteraction of destructive speculation. It can do so only, however, if there is not a fundamental disequilibrium; its function is one of bridging temporary gaps. It cannot bridge permanent gaps.

CHAPTER V

DISEQUILIBRIUM AND EQUILIBRIUM
IN THE BALANCE OF PAYMENTS

v.1. In this chapter some consequences of disequilibrium in the balance of payments will be considered; the conditions for equilibrium will be formulated and some techniques of short-term adaptations discussed.

In a state of *multilateral payments equilibrium* between nations there will be equality between the payments any country has to make to other countries and the receipts it has to expect from other countries. This does not necessarily imply, as we discussed already, bilateral equilibrium between any two countries. Country A may have to pay more to country B than country B to country A; there will, then, be a deficit of country A with regard to country B in bilateral intercourse. But if they have 'overall' equilibrium, A will have a surplus with some other country and B a deficit, and both can use their surpluses to pay for their deficits. In such a situation there will be no difficulty to declare any currency fully convertible into any other; demand for and supply of each currency are equal to each other.

v.2. This easy situation vanishes if the balances of payments are *not* in *equilibrium*. Even then convertibility may for some time be maintained, if all countries are in the possession of gold or equivalent reserves. In a situation of disequilibrium there will be surplus and deficit countries. The reserves of the former will increase, and those of the latter decrease and finally get exhausted. After this exhaustion the currency of the country concerned will no longer be convertible at the existing rate of exchange. Certain portions of the demand for foreign currency can no longer be satisfied and the currency will be '*soft*' as distinguished from the '*hard*' currencies of the surplus countries. Convertibility could — perhaps — be restored if the exchange rate was lowered, i.e. the price of one unit of that currency in terms of the others was lowered. The ratio of this equilibrium rate to the actual rate may be considered a measure of the 'degree of softness' of the currency concerned. The possibility to define this degree depends on the existence of an equilibrium rate; we will assume this to exist, although under certain circumstances such an equilibrium rate might not be attainable in the short run. In order not to disorganize international economic intercourse completely, payments of a soft currency will have to be regulated; this means that certain demands for foreign currency will have to be cut off by '*currency regulations*'; these are, in their material consequences, equivalent to quota systems imposed on trade. An important example of a complicated set of regulations was supplied by the monetary organization of the Sterling Area after World War II, of which a simplified scheme is given in table VII.

v.3. After a *disturbance of pre-existing equilibria* as for example caused by a war, a currency may be soft for some time because of a fall in general productivity of the country or because of exceptional demand (as far as financed by inflationary means). With a gradual restoration of productivity and of a sound internal financial situation, the question may come up whether convertibility can be restored, perhaps even at the pre-existing rates. For tempo-

TABLE VII

TRANSFERABILITY OF STERLING FOR DIRECT CURRENT TRANSACTIONS AMONG NON-STERLING, NON-DOLLAR COUNTRIES

To / *From*	Members of Transferable Accounts Area and E.P.U.[1]	Members of Transferable Accounts Area but not E.P.U.[2]	Members of Bilateral Group and E.P.U.[3]	Members of Bilateral Group but not E.P.U.[4]
Members of Transferable Accounts Area *and* E.P.U.	Yes	Yes	Yes	No
Members of Transferable Accounts Area but *not* E.P.U.	Yes	Yes	No	No
Members of Bilateral Group *and* E.P.U.	Yes	No	Yes	No
Members of Bilateral Group but *not* E.P.U.	No	No	No	No

Key to membership of each group:

[1] Austria, Denmark, German Federal Republic, Greece, Italian Monetary Area, Netherlands Monetary Area, Norway, Sweden.

[2] Sudan, Chile, Czechoslovakia, Egypt, Ethiopia, Finland, Poland, Spanish Monetary Area, Thailand, U.S.S.R.

[3] Belgian Monetary Area, French Franc Area, Portuguese Monetary Area, Switzerland, Turkey.

[4] Argentina, Brazil, Bulgaria, China, Hungary, Iran, Israel, Japan, Lebanon, Paraguay, Peru, Rumania, Syria, Tangier, Uruguay, Vatican City, Yugoslavia.

Source: J. R. Sargent, 'Convertibility', Oxford Economic Papers 6 (1954) p. 55.

rary disturbances this is likely to be so; and this likelihood is one of the reasons why regulations are applied during the period of softness. Another reason may be that there is no certainty about the existence of a short-run equilibrium rate.

In order to answer the important question whether, in the circumstances just indicated, the moment has come to *re-establish convertibility*, the conditions have to be found which should be fulfilled in order that it can persist. Evidently these conditions are dependent on the exact type of convertibility envisaged. Usually it will be, in one or more respects, *partial* convertibility which is aimed at. It may be partial in that only some groups of transactions are involved, e.g. only current transactions and not capital transactions. Or it may be partial because convertibility in some other but not all other currencies is aimed at. Evidently the relevant conditions are that demand for and supply of the currencies with which convertibility is restored should be equal. This demand and supply refer to the items in the balance of payments bearing on the *currencies and type of transactions concerned, under the new circumstances*. The 'new circumstances' are on the one hand that the currency restrictions are now eliminated and that 'free' demand and supply should be estimated; on the other hand they imply certain shifts in transactions likely to occur as a consequence of convertibility. These consequences may even be the re-imposition of certain trade restrictions if it was felt that otherwise demand for foreign currency might rise too much.

v.4. The concepts just mentioned may be somewhat more specified by considering in some more detail the balance of payments of the country concerned. The items of that

balance may be subdivided according to two criteria simultaneously, namely, whether referring to countries S with
which there is a surplus or countries D with which there
is a deficit and whether referring to countries C with which
convertibility is to be restored or to countries N with which
it is not to be restored. It will be assumed that the type of
convertibility envisaged is to make the country's money
convertible into *currencies themselves already convertible
into gold* (to call 'convertible money'). This is not the only
type of convertibility conceivable. Let the net transactions
with the four groups be as indicated in the table below,
where a and c therefore represent surpluses and b and d
deficits:

Net transactions (before convertibility)

with countries	S(urplus)	D(eficit)
C(onvertible)	$+a$	$-b$
N(on-convertible)	$+c$	$-d$

Before convertibility the country considered receives a in
convertible money (say dollars, for convenience's sake)
and c in non-convertible (say soft) money, i.e. in money not
yet convertible in \$. After convertibility the country will
again receive a in \$ and c in soft money. Before converti-
bility it paid b in \$ but d in soft money; after convertibility
it will have to pay, as a maximum, both in \$. Primarily there
is a disadvantage therefore which is exactly the point at
stake: an amount d may have to be paid in \$ now. This
disadvantage is the smaller, the smaller group N is, i.e. the
larger the group of countries which, together with the
country considered, also plan to make their currency convertible. In a way the condition to be fulfilled therefore
is that the country can supply an extra amount of d in \$.

There are, however, other consequences to be taken into

account. The country's own currency, say guilders, will be in higher demand as a consequence of the considered convertibility. This means that there will be a tendency for foreign countries to supply commodities at a somewhat lower price and to demand somewhat less products. This will change the balance of payments, be it in an unknown direction. In addition, and partly in response to the tendency just described, a tendency for the country studied to introduce further restrictions on trade with country N will develop, since this will reduce the obligation to supply dollars to those countries.

v.5. The above analysis may have exemplified how to judge the conditions that have to be fulfilled in order to warrant persistency. It will also be clear that the risks involved in complete convertibility, i.e. including capital items, are far larger than those involved in convertibility on current items only. Especially the switches in capital assets that the public may desire to perform are very difficult to foresee. Some of these risks have been demonstrated by the attempt in 1947 to make sterling convertible. The attempt was unsuccessful and had to be discontinued because of too heavy drains on the gold stock of the Sterling Area.

A last remark on convertibility we want to make is that the decisions taken by different countries should be *consistent* one with the other: convertibility of currency A into currency B and of B into C has to imply convertibility of A into C also; there have to be groups of mutually convertible currencies and these should be of about equal strength.

v.6. Since it will be clear that universal convertibility, which is a great advantage for international trade, is only possible if *balance of payments equilibrium* is warranted, we will now consider somewhat more closely the conditions for such equilibrium and the instruments that may be used to attain or to maintain it. Balance of payments equilibrium is the financial expression of an equilibrium in the 'real' economic sphere, i.e. in production and trade.

We will discuss, in succession, the *general characteristics* of an equilibrated situation and the *possibilities*, in concrete situations, to *attain and maintain equilibrium*.

Equilibrium in the balance of payments of any country is *equivalent to equality between total income and total expenditure*. This equivalence is most easily understood as a consequence of the definition of income of a national economy. In order to fix the ideas we have to specify the nature of the economy; but our conclusion will not depend on that nature. We will assume that imports are only imports of raw materials and semi-finished articles; in a way this is always correct, since it may be maintained that practically no article at the moment of importation is finished in the economic sense of the word: it has almost always to pass some stage of trade at least. This assumption means that the nation's expenditures (i.e. its spending of income) only consists of expenditures to nationals. Indicating now by:

Y — the nation's income
X — total expenditure
E — exports of goods and services
M — imports of goods and services

the definition of income runs:

$$Y = X + E - M$$

In fact, $X + E$ represent the *gross value of all production*,

83

M the costs of the nation's production and hence their difference represents income. The word gross should be specified, since it has different meanings; it does not, in our case, mean gross as far as investment expenditure is concerned. If so, we would have to deduct depreciation as a separate item, and the definition would then run

$$Y = X' + E - N - M$$

where X' is expenditure including gross investments and N is depreciation allowances.

The formula may be written in a different way:

$$X - Y = M - E$$

telling that the excess, if any, of expenditure over income equals the excess of imports over exports (in the widest sense), or the import surplus. It follows that equality between E and M implies equality between Y and X, or, as it is sometimes called, *monetary equilibrium*. In the absence of monetary equilibrium, the figure $X - Y$ will be called the *inflationary gap*, if it is positive; if it is negative, the positive figure $Y - X$ will be called the *deflationary gap*.

An important gap between Y and X can only exist for countries with a considerable portion of foreign trade. In a closed country (and hence for the world as a whole), Y will always, by its definition, be equal to X, since X has to be spent completely inside the country and an increase in X will therefore result in an increase in Y. The criterion for monetary equilibrium just given therefore is less practical for big countries; one would have to be very precise about the time lag between Y and X in order to apply it correctly. What should be compared is X with the value of Y shortly before. If one compared simultaneous values of X and Y they would always be equal; if the volume of production cannot adapt itself to X, the price level will do the rest of the adaptation. For a big country a more practical criterion will therefore be the *constancy of prices*, which in its turn would be an inaccurate criterion for small countries: the latter cannot influence the price level much and will never raise prices if even X exceeds Y by much.

This *equivalence between balance of payments equilibrium and monetary equilibrium for small countries* is very important since most countries are, in this sense, small. It implies that one certain way of attaining balance of payments equilibrium is to make national expenditure equal to national income or 'to live within the limits set by income'. One should, nevertheless, be careful in using this formula; changes in expenditure very often cause changes in income and an attempt to cut expenditures may not always lead to the expected effect. We will come back to this point below. Be it sufficient for the moment to say that the country can regulate the *autonomous part of its expenditure*, not the part which depends on its income.

Apart from it, there is the other characteristic of equilibrium which matters, namely, *the level of production* and hence of employment, with which it corresponds. Equilibrium in the wider sense implies a volume of production where no productive agents are unused, or only a small portion which may be necessary as a reserve for effectuating shifts. This is especially desirable for labour and is equivalent to '*high and stable employment*'. Since with a higher level of production also a higher level of imports corresponds, high production requires high imports and, because of equilibrium in the balance of payments, also high exports. The latter have to be saleable if they are at all to be obtained and the condition of a high-level equilibrium, therefore, is that *prices are sufficiently low* to make exports saleable. Prices are thus the second important factor, alongside with national expenditure, whose level has to obey a certain condition if equilibrium at a high level is to be realised.

v.7. It should be realised that the position of equilibrium as specified in the previous section is one of *equilibrium relatively to other countries*. In order that the set of all countries be in equilibrium, they have all to satisfy the conditions indicated, namely, that their balance of payments be in equilibrium and that their price level be 'in line with the world market'. Now if we have a 'world' of say ten countries, there are ten balance of payments surpluses (positive or negative), but of these only nine are independent from each other. The tenth must always add up with the nine other to zero since, by definition, there cannot be a surplus or deficit for the world as a whole. Therefore the ten figures of the autonomous expenditures of the ten countries are not all of them relevant to what will happen to the balances of payments. It is only their relative level which matters: nine relative figures determine the nine balance of payments gaps. They may, in addition, 'blow up' their absolute expenditures without affecting their balances of payments. Such 'blowing up' will lead, for the world as a whole, to higher levels of production, as long as there are idle resources, and to higher absolute prices, if full employment has been reached. If the latter phase were attained there may be said to be 'inflation' in the world at large — as in war time — without any balances of payments being in disequilibrium or more in disequilibrium than before. Also, the price levels may be kept 'in line' with each other, and nonetheless all may rise. In such a process small countries can only more or less follow the others; a 'world inflation' can only be avoided by a concerted action or possibly by some of the large countries.

It also follows that a disruption of equilibrium in a small country may either be 'due' to the country's own policy or to the policy of other countries. In this connection we may speak of *'imported' inflation* and *'exported' inflation*. By the former term we understand the price rise in a small country which occurs as a consequence of excessive expenditures elsewhere, causing import prices of the small country to rise; an exported inflation of a small country being a deficit on that country's balance of payments caused by its own excessive expenditure. This latter may not lead to a price rise (small countries can hardly influence world market prices), especially if the balance of payments deficit can be financed. The small countries have the disadvantage of being exposed to imported inflation, without being able to prevent it, but they have the advantage of being able to 'export' their own inflation, in this sense, as long as they have reserves or as long as they are granted credits.

v.8. Having formulated the conditions for balance of payments equilibrium in a general way, we are now going to discuss some possibilities of adaptation in case of disruption of equilibrium. The adaptations to be discussed are those in the realm of national expenditure and price fixation as distinct from the adaptation in the sphere of the central bank, discussed in chapter IV. As already indicated, these adaptations take somewhat more time; the quickest may act after a few months and some ultimate consequences may only occur after years. Apart from short-term capital transfers which have already been discussed in ch. IV and apart from long-term capital transfers which have been discussed in ch. III, and will be considered as given for the moment, maintenance of balance of payments equilibrium means equality in changes of imports and exports in the widest sense, i.e. of commodities and services. If disrupted, the equilibrium will have to be restored by reductions or increases in one or both of these items. The question thus arises how such adaptations can be obtained. The following discussion may be seen as an application of the general remarks just made on the determinants of the balance of payments. For both imports and exports it may be said, as is true of the transactions in any market, that changes may be the consequences of

(1) autonomous changes in demand or supply, without changes in price ratios or absolute prices, and

(2) changes in price ratios, inducing changes in quantities demanded or supplied.

Autonomous changes may be exemplified, on the demand side, i.e. with imports, by reductions in the autonomous expenditures of the nation. Usually these are supposed to be certain investment expenditures and certain state expenditures; partly they are also certain expenditures for consumption. Their common characteristic is their independence from income or prices. If they are reduced, a reduction in import demand will also result. Autonomous reductions in imports may also be obtained, to some extent, by the application of quantitative restrictions (also called quotas). Their net extent is not necessarily equal to the direct restrictions applied, since income may seek other outlets. This is why either an almost complete system of import quotas or reductions in income will be needed. If the former policy is not desired, reductions in income will

88

be the only way; and these can only be obtained by reductions in autonomous expenditure, being the determinant of income.

Autonomous changes on the supply side may be effectuated by rises in productive capacity, leading to increased supplies of export commodities. In the long run these changes will be the most satisfactory ones since they increase rather than restrict production and the standard of life. In the short run their influence will only be restricted since they require new investments and these are limited to a rather modest portion of national income.

v.9. Changes in *price ratios* are the other road towards an adjustment in the balance of payments. They may take the form either of

(i) direct changes in absolute prices of certain commodities, or

(ii) indirect changes, i.e. changes obtained by changes in wage level or rates of exchange.

There are two important sets of problems connected with their application. First, it may be asked whether they are *at all necessary;* secondly, whether, if necessary, they *do work.* They may not be necessary if the changes in autonomous demand and supply which have caused disequilibrium or are feared to cause disequilibrium do themselves already restore equilibrium; or if other changes in autonomous demand or supply are the normal method to overcome disequilibrium. There has been much discussion about the first question — whether price changes are at all necessary — in connection with two topics. One was the influence of capital exports or imports on the balances of payments of the countries concerned; the other the influence of reparation payments required from Germany after the First World War. The general reason why, under certain conditions, no price adaptations would be necessary, is that the shifts in autonomous demand connected with the transfer discussed would by themselves be just sufficient to offset these transfers. Such appears to be the case, upon closer investigation, if the behaviour of the nation is 'classical' in the Keynesian sense, i.e. if the nation spends an increase in disposible resources completely. If the spending behaviour, however, was Keynesian, i.e. not the complete increase in resources would be spent, a disequilibrium in the balance of payments will remain which will have to be eliminated in another way.

Even if the shifts in financial resources which are the origin of a disequilibrium have not, by themselves, already brought about the adaptation in demand, it may be judged that they will do so in the long run or that the most natural return to equilibrium will be another change in autonomous demand or supply, as discussed before.

But there are circumstances under which autonomous changes cannot be hoped for or would have undesirable consequences for, say, the volume of employment. Then the second question becomes relevant, namely, whether changes in price ratios, i.e. in the ratios between national and international prices will be able to do the job. This depends on the reaction of imports and exports to such changes.

v.10. The total *influence of a change in price ratios* on the balance of payments consists of three components: (i) a change in the volume of imports; (ii) a change in the volume of exports; and (iii) a change in the terms of trade. A fall in national prices in relation to foreign ones will raise the volume of exports and so influence the balance of payments favourably. Its influence on the volume of imports is composed of two opposite effects; the rise in export volume will raise the volume of imports also; but the price change will tend to reduce it. The outcome depends on various elasticities. Finally, the influence on the terms of trade will be unfavourable to the balance of payments. Since the different partial effects involved are of opposite signs, the total effect may be negative, zero, or positive. If it is negative, zero or slightly positive, it will be insufficient. The case where it is exactly zero is called the case of *'critical elasticities';* under certain further assumptions this is the situation if the sum total of the price elasticities of exports and imports equals one. If the elasticities happen to be in the neighbourhood of this situation, price ratio changes cannot therefore help to restore payments equilibrium. Even if they are considerably higher, the response of the balance of payments to changes in price ratios that are within the realm of practical possibilities may be insufficient. This is the case for quantitative restrictions as the only way out of balance of payments difficulties.

The elasticities to which this applies are rather low. There is some evidence that such elasticities actually exist, although opinions among statisticians diverge rather widely. There is quite some evidence, however, that in the long run elasticities will be considerably higher. It may be, therefore, that the critical situation only applies or nearly applies to short-term reactions. This would mean that quantitative restrictions would only be needed as a temporary device and could, afterwards, be removed.

Even if changes in price ratios worked, as far as elasticities of demand and supply are concerned, another question may arise, namely, how to obtain such changes. Direct changes in absolute prices of export products cannot be set by governments in a free economy. If only indirect influencing of these prices is considered feasible, the question is whether the available instruments, namely wage changes and changes in exchange rates, will have the desired effects. Also here situations may occur, where no sufficient response is obtained, since there are other consequences to be expected in addition to those aimed at. A wage change cannot surpass a certain limit and may for that reason be insufficient. A change in the rate of exchange will have consequences for the internal price and wage level and it depends on their extent whether the net effect is sufficient. Statistical investigations have shown, in this case also, that under boom conditions changes in exchange rates do not alter price ratios of national to foreign prices. Here again quantitative restrictions are the only way out. The two cases therefore where either elasticities are low, or price changes cannot be large enough represent cases in which such restrictions are justified; they are the basis for what was called the British 'austerity policy' under the Labour government after the Second World War.

SECOND PART

INTERNATIONAL ECONOMIC INTEGRATION

Chapter VI

TARGETS AND INSTRUMENTS OF INTERNATIONAL ECONOMIC INTEGRATION

VI.I. In the preceding five chapters we have dealt with the essence of international economic relations between autonomous nations. We have also tried to clarify the mechanism of these relations by discussing certain possibilities to change them. After having thus indicated the possibilities to regulate them, we shall now discuss how far we want to regulate them. Such regulation, when aimed at more systematically, is nowadays usually called '*integration*' of the various national economies. Integration may be said to be the creation of the most desirable structure of international economy, removing artificial hindrances to the optimal operation and introducing deliberately all desirable elements of co-ordination or unification. The problem of integration therefore forms part of a more general problem, namely that of the *optimum economic policy*. When making recommendations on economic policy we are actually leaving the territory of objective science or at least introducing outside elements. Since a good deal of economic analysis will have to be used nevertheless we will warn the reader every time such extra-economic elements are being used.

VI.2. It is useful to make some *general remarks* on the field of *economic policy* before embarking upon our special case of integration. Economic policy will be taken to mean the activity of public authorities as such in the economic field.

95

It therefore excludes the activity of public authorities as producers or consumers, as far as the normal aims of production and consumption are concerned. As soon as more general aims are involved policy begins. There are greatly differing types of policy, however. A first distinction may be made between *qualitative* and *quantitative* policy. By an act of qualitative economic policy we mean every change in the organization or structure of society, as far as of economic importance. By acts of quantitative economic policy we mean changes in the data controlled by public authorities, within an unchanged framework of organization. Examples of changes in organization may be the introduction of a monopoly by law, the dissolution of a monopoly, changes in property rights or the introduction of a new international agency. Examples of changes in data within a given organization are changes in tax rates, in public expenditure, or in the rate of discount of the Central Bank. Data are partly under the control of public authorities, as in the cases just quoted; these will be called *instruments* or instrument variables. The other data are not under the control of public authorities, such as weather conditions, population growth, or technical development.

Some of the most frequently used instruments have been mentioned already: taxes, public expenditure, and the rate of discount. They could be specified and others could be added. A number of examples will be given below.

There are wide differences in the scope and extent of either type of policy: both may be far-reaching or modest in scope. Fundamental qualitative policies may be called *reforms* or even *revolutions* if they change the structure of society in important points; but there may also be modest changes in organization, such as the introduction of collective bargaining or the establishment of a new tax. Also quantitative policies may be far-reaching or modest. In a depression very important public expenditures may be added or tax reductions applied; in a situation near monetary equilibrium only slight changes in some tax rates may be considered. Quantitative policy in a country with extensive government intervention may use a large number of instruments, say rationing applied to a large number of commodities, detailed price regulations and so on; whereas quantitative policy in a laissez-faire country may have a very limited number of taxes to manipulate.

In the field of quantitative policies a distinction can be made between *direct* and *indirect intervention;* the former being the direct interference with market forces such as rationing and price setting. Important instruments from the international point of view are the ones directly affecting foreign trade: import duties, quantitative restrictions on imports, or currency regulations. Indirect intervention operates before all through *financial policy* (credit as well as fiscal policy). It goes without saying that the introduction of some new type of intervention by itself represents an act of qualitative policy; once it exists, however, the changes in rations, prices etc., are only of a quantitative character. As always there may be borderline cases.

VI.3. An important aspect of acts of qualitative policy is the choice between *centralization* and *decentralization* or rather the choice of the degree of centralization. This choice has to be made inside each country as well as in international economic policy. Inside each country certain functions of economic life will be performed more efficiently when organized centrally while others may better be decentralized. The same problem shows itself in private business as

97

well as in extra-economic — political, cultural and social — activities. Centralization or decentralization may be defined in the *geographical* sense as well as in the *'functional'* sense: certain activities may be left to lower public authorities — which would be an example of geographical decentralization — or to specialized private organs, each of them national, but acting only in a restricted type of functions. In a way the question of the most desirable economic policy — in particular as far as intervention by public authorities is concerned — may be said to be the very question of what degree of decentralization in economic activities is most healthy. Private enterprise is an example of decentralization.

The main topic of this part of the present book — international economic integration — is intimately connected with the question of decentralization and centralization. The question that will have to be answered is precisely: Which functions in international economic life should be subject to central control and which should be left to individual countries, enterprises or persons?

Some general remarks and *formal directives* may already be given before even the aim of economic policy is specified.

Since economic policy means the handling of instruments by policy-makers it seems to be natural that the degree of centralization wanted will to a large extent depend on the nature of their effect on the well-being of each of the countries concerned. According to their effects instruments may be of four types. If a certain change in an instrument acts in the same direction on the well-being of all countries concerned, it will be called *supporting*, since the use of such an instrument by one country will support the policies of the other countries. If a change in an instrument used by country A acts in opposite directions inside and outside that country, the instrument will be called *conflicting*: its use by country A conflicts with the objectives of other countries' policies. If the instrument does not act at all on the well-being of other countries, we will call it *neutral*. Finally there will be instruments acting in a mixed way, to be called *mixed* instruments.

An example of a supporting instrument is the level of government expenditure in a general depression or in the case of general inflation: in both cases their effect will be parallel for all countries concerned. In times of depression an increase in government expenditure in any country will be acting favourably on all countries; and in times of inflation a decrease in public expenditure in one country will be wholesome for the other countries as well. An example of a conflicting instrument in case of a general depression is the rate of exchange of any one country. Its lowering will affect the country itself favourably but the other countries, as a rule, unfavourably. Examples of neutral instruments will be instruments of a local character only. The effects of most instruments will depend on circumstances; this is why the distinction made is formal only. The instrument of government expenditures will act in a mixed way, for instance, if certain countries are in an inflationary situation and others in a deflationary situation.

In general there is a strong case for decentralization since it means freedom to groups or individuals which constitutes an element of direct satisfaction. In addition it may avoid costs.

vi.4. Apart from this general argument in favour of decentralization there will be arguments in favour of centralization, primarily applying to the first two types of instruments, for the reason that the other countries have a strong interest in their handling. This interest is parallel in the case of supporting instruments and opposed in the case of conflicting instruments. The aim of centralization in these two cases will therefore be different: centralized decisions on supporting instruments will tend to *intensify* their use, whereas centralized use of conflicting instruments will tend to *eliminate* or *mitigate* their use. The disadvantages of centralization will only be compensated by important advantages if the character of the instruments under discussion is of an outspoken supporting or of a clearly conflicting character.

In less outspoken cases, i.e. in any case when the instrument is neutral, and often if it has mixed consequences, there is more to be said in favour of decentralization.

VI.5. The *choice of the instruments* of economic policy has to be made dependent on a number of circumstances. It goes without saying that the nature of the problems to be solved will have to be taken account of. This is particularly true for the extent of the problems. The same problem when presenting itself in a modest size may be solvable with modest means but when showing an extraordinary extent may require more fundamental acts. War-time disturbances and similar emergency situations usually require more direct interventions than smaller and more temporary disturbances. During and after the latter sufficient help may be expected from the automatic reactions of economic life. A short supply in only one crop will be followed by a price rise which automatically diverts demand to other products and so solves the difficulty. A general shortage of food cannot be remedied in this way since a general price rise will not divert demand sufficiently.

Apart from the nature and the extent of the problems to

be solved by any form of economic policy the choice of instruments will depend on certain *pre-conceived ideas* of which the extreme examples are *complete regulation* on the one and *complete absence of it* on the other hand. These ideas themselves cannot be divorced from the aims of economic policy, to be discussed hereafter. Historically it may be said that the tendency towards freedom was largest when political power was in the hands of business leaders and that the tendency towards complete regulation exists with military and with communist groups as leading politicians. It cannot be denied that greater emphasis on the interests of the masses sometimes requires more intervention; but it is also probable that the necessity of intervention tends to be overemphasized by those anxious to exert power for its own sake and as a reaction to a lack of power in the past. It is the serious task of economics and sociology to try to find objective criteria for the choice of instruments as often as possible. Some attempts will be found in this text.

VI.6. The relevance of any acts of economic policy depends on the *targets* or *aims* set. The choice of these aims, or *objectives of economic policy* is itself extra-economic, just as the aim of each individual in economic matters cannot be explained by economic reasoning but has to be considered as given. Whereas, however, the objectives one man aims at may, as a rule, be left to himself as long as he does not definitely interfere with the interests of others, the setting of aims to the economic policy of a community of different individuals involves difficult problems. A well-known formula for the goal to be aimed at is the pursuance of a '*maximum welfare*' for the community, or the furtherance of the '*general interest*', but upon closer consideration these formulae are 'empty boxes' unless further specified.

Human welfare is affected by different elements of which the most important, from the economic point of view, seem to be

(a) those referring to *individual well-being* namely the availability of goods and of leisure, and

(b) those referring to man's *relations to other individuals* namely freedom, justice and peace.

These are solemn words and the reader should excuse them and consider them as a very brief indication of some of the most important complexes of the relevant elements. Also, the list is not exhaustive; and the valuation of the various elements varies in time and diverges between individuals. Some individuals sometimes like the opposites of justice and peace.

If individuals could live independently one of the other the elements under (b) might not come into play and each could strive for his individual optimum of goods and leisure, it usually being so that more goods can only be had if less leisure is accepted. Several circumstances, however, make for mutual dependence of individuals. The bare fact of vicinity introduces the possibility of conflicts and the elements under (b) come into play. This is reinforced very much by the technical possibilities of increasing production opened up by co-operation in the production process. These two forms of dependence make the problem of economic policy extremely complicated, especially because of the inequality in individual capacities and tastes. They destroy the possibility for each individual to strive for his own optimum; common decisions have to be taken and the decisions one individual would prefer differ from those desired by others. They differ because of varying tastes, differences in insight and wisdom and plain divergency of interests. So far no generally accepted method has been found to reconcile these differences. To be specific and to give an important example, no method is available to decide whether a transfer of one dollar from Mr A to Mr B means an increase in welfare or a decrease. It is much more difficult to say whether a transfer of $ 1 milliard from country A to country B implies an increase in general welfare or not. Still more difficult are choices between more or fewer regulations (which may increase justice but will decrease freedom) or between a strike and its avoidance (the strike may bring greater justice, but it breaks peace). Unfortunately even international peace seems to have a restricted value to certain governments.

At this stage of our knowledge and insight an accurate and generally acceptable formulation is only possible for a few aims of economic policy, whereas other aims cannot so be formulated. A relatively high degree of agreement exists about the '*aims of high production*', i.e. the aims (1) of using all productive resources, and (2) using them in the most efficient way, since the interests of individuals in this respect are largely parallel. Difficulties arise as soon as questions of *distribution* are considered, because of differences about the meaning of justice. Only to the extent that distribution indirectly affects efficiency, more possibilities of agreement arise.

Difficulties also arise as to the *choice of the instruments of economic policy*, the main dilemma then being the one between freedom on the one hand, and the aims (1) and (2), as well as justice on the other hand.

Agreement on these aims is only possible in very outspoken cases; on measures towards a more equal distribution e.g. if the existing inequality is very strong, and agreement on the use of instruments of detailed intervention only if very strong disequilibria are threatening society.

Briefly therefore the main groups of aims of economic policy may be formulated in the following way:

(1) the use of *all productive resources* implying the *avoidance of instability* in production;

(2) the use of these resources in the *most efficient* way;

(3) a more *equal distribution* of incomes between persons and between countries as far as there is strong inequality, and

(4) the use of *instruments of detailed intervention only in order to prevent strong disequilibria.*

It is in accordance with the above argument that even this formulation contains concepts that are only vaguely determined; at best it could be added that what is understood by 'strong inequality' and 'strong disequilibrium' depends on the development of public opinion and will as a rule be defined by political decisions in the more general sense.

Notwithstanding this restricted set of more or less accepted aims it is remarkable that a relatively well-defined set of rules of economic policy can be derived. This is due to the fact that economic life is permanently threatened by disruptions of equilibrium by variations in crops, new inventions and political events and that the skilful maintenance of equilibrium is already a complicated art of considerable importance to general well-being. In addition the inherent tendency towards strong inequalities is so clear that permanent redistribution with a minimum loss of efficiency is the other main technique required.

VI.7. If it is true that a certain concensus of opinion prevails on the general aims formulated above, it cannot be denied that the big differences in economic policies between the non-communist and the communist countries — already referred to in section VI.5. — can only partly be explained in this way. It is true that inequalities in the latter countries were larger than in many Western countries and it is true that the disturbances created by the first world war in Russia and by the second world war in the present communist area were large indeed. But there are other countries where this also applies and these countries are not — or shall we say: not yet — communist. Certain differences in history, in national character and in political aspirations — and some pure co-incidences — have also to be accepted as part of the explanation.

The fact of the existence of the two political blocks has unfortunately to be considered largely a datum to present-day problems of economic policy. The time where it could have been avoided by a wiser economic policy (in the widest sense) seems to have passed. There are, thus, wide divergencies in basic economic organization. This also necessarily affects international relations. Centrally organized or at least highly interventionist countries will also show centrally organized or highly regulated international relations. Similarly, less strongly organized countries will prefer less organized international relations. In their inter-course with the first group they will be forced, nevertheless, to organize contacts to some extent also on their part, if only to create the 'opposite numbers' to the civil servants of the centralized countries in the necessary discussions, negociations and executive measures. They may, on the other hand, bring in decentralized elements in the execution inside their own countries to the extent they think desirable. In other terms, international relations between countries of different political structure necessarily will have to be dependent on these national structures and in a way represent some transitory form. The more decentralized countries cannot choose their relations with centralized countries freely. These relations will not be discussed to any great extent in this book, since political elements will be much more decisive in the first few years to come than will economic factors.

International relations between the more decentralized countries themselves, however, can be shaped more deliberately and therefore according to the principles commonly adhered to by these countries. It is mainly with these relations that we are going to deal in the next chapters.

vi.8. Turning now to the problem of *integration* as a special aspect of international economic policy we are going to discuss this according to the groups of instruments of economic policy. We distinguish two main groups, namely those commonly considered as *national instruments* and those seen as *international ones*. The latter are the instruments directly affecting international transactions; all the other ones will be grouped into the former category. By so doing we are paying a tribute to tradition rather than applying a thorough analysis; the very problem being exactly to what extent national instruments should remain sovereign national instruments. In chapter VII national economic policies will be considered in their relation to integration; the instruments considered being mainly the indirect ones of financial policy and the instruments determining the general price level. As a subsidiary group certain specified taxes will be considered. In chapter VIII the non-monetary instruments and in chapter IX the monetary instruments directly affecting international transactions will be treated.

Chapter X deals with the integration of development and in a concluding chapter the agencies of international economic co-operation will be very briefly discussed.

CHAPTER VII

NATIONAL ECONOMIC POLICIES AND INTERNATIONAL INTEGRATION

VII.I. The relations between the more decentralized countries of the non-communist world may be shaped, as we saw, according to the principles adhered to by these countries. We tried to formulate the general principles on which their economic policy is based in chapter VI. The problem how to regulate the international relations between these countries should be seen, as will be clear from that chapter, as part of the more general problem of the economic policy of these countries in its totality. The best setting of the coherent groups of problems involved would seem to be: *how should economic policy as a whole* — both 'national' and 'international' — *be organized* in order to attain the goals enumerated in the best manner? By so setting the problem we see that on the one hand national and on the other hand international policies should both show the optimum degree of decentralization. This means that part of the 'national' instruments should just as well be submitted to a certain international co-ordination as certain instruments of international policy, whereas, on the other hand, certain other instruments of international economic policy might just as well be left decentralized as a number of instruments of internal policy. To quote a concrete example of the latter: international trade will be left largely, if not entirely, in private hands, as will the majority of internal transactions. Only some 'strategic' instruments will be handled by the authorities, such as the rate of exchange, possibly certain import duties, etc. in international policy and taxes, public expenditures, etc. in internal policy. It may prove that some of these instruments had better be handled in a centralized way by the international community. And this class is not necessarily restricted to the instruments of international economic policy. This chapter deals with the need for centralization in handling certain instruments of national economic policy.

VII.2. From the foregoing chapter will be clear that the instruments of national, or internal, policy for which this is true are in particular those that have a *conflicting* or a *supporting character*. Whether instruments have one of these characteristics depends, we know, on the influence they exert on other countries' welfare. Of the main instruments of internal economic policy mentioned in chapter VI those who influence the general level of activity will also influence other countries' welfare to a considerable extent. Instruments influencing the distribution of income between groups or individuals will make themselves felt to a much lesser degree in foreign countries: they will not, as a rule, affect total imports or even imports from certain countries so much.

The aim of influencing the general level of activity will be usually formulated in the wording: *maintenance of monetary equilibrium at a high level of employment*. To maintain monetary equilibrium is equivalent — as we saw in chapter V — to the maintenance of balance between total income and total expenditure, or, again, to the avoidance of the use of 'inflationary financing' for the country as a whole, i.e. for the total of private and public income and expenditure. The exact meaning of the term 'inflationary financing' will be discussed below. In principle, however, monetary equilibrium is possible — as we also discussed in chapter V — at different levels of employment. Maintaining monetary equilibrium at a low level of employment would mean maintaining stagnation, and to fix demand of imports as well as domestic demand at a lower level than is possible with the country's resources. This is why the second part of the aim was formulated as a high-employment level of monetary equilibrium.

While therefore the use of inflation as a permanent instrument of economic policy is undesirable, attaining high employment from an initial position of low employment may require the temporary use of credit creation. It should also be kept in mind that a regular increase of the money supply of a country in order to meet the increased demand for liquidity at constant prices does not mean inflation in this context. Inflation, according to the definition adhered to here, would be the creation of more money than is needed for financing high-employment production at the desired price level plus financing increased liquidity holdings.

It is not always easy to avoid, at least temporarily, the use of inflationary financing. It may happen that in a period of 'high liquidity preference' (i.e. when people want to hold ample liquid reserves) more money is needed to maintain high and stable employment than in a subsequent period of lower liquidity preference. The presence of ample cash reserves may induce people, once they no longer prefer to hold reserves to that extent, to spend more than their current income and so to cause a boom and inflationary price rises. Under such circumstances taxes should be increased or attractive loans made in order to 'drain' circulation. The policy of high and stable employment therefore has not only to watch income flows but also the composition and use made of assets.

VII.3. There are *two groups* of *main instruments* for this policy and a number of *subsidiary* ones. The first main group is that of financial policy, consisting of public expenditure policy and tax policy. By an appropriate manipulation of these instruments total internal demand will be kept at the desired level and its composition may be made optimal.

The level may be influenced by public expenditures as well as by taxes. If a decline in private demand occurs, e.g. as a consequence of decreased investments, public demand may be increased by higher expenditures. But stimulating private expenditure may also be attempted by a lowering of taxes. It may therefore depend on the *composition of total national expenditure* that is desired whether more emphasis should be laid on one instrument or the other. If important public investment projects are available, the first line may be followed; if however, there are only projects of low priority it may be a better use of the country's resources to stimulate private demand.

Once a tax reduction is preferred to increased public expenditure, the further question arises *which taxes* should be reduced. The first choice may be between direct and indirect taxes. Indirect taxes will influence consumption probably more than an equal change in direct taxes. If more consumption is considered desirable, there may therefore be a case for decreasing indirect taxes. Even investment may be stimulated in this case, if lack of sales kept them down rather than lack of financial means. If, on the other hand, private investment was low because of lack of finance, a reduction in direct taxes may be more appropriate. In times of depression, a reduction in direct taxes might, however, lead to increased hoarding rather than to increased expenditure and then would be less efficient as an instrument of economic policy.

After a decision has been taken as to the general category of taxes that should be lowered, there is another choice to be made about precisely which of the individual taxes be chosen. We are coming back to this question when discussing the situation in individual industries.

VII.4. First we will discuss the *second group of main instruments* of internal economic policy. They refer to the general level of *prices, wages* and *other income rates*. This group of economic variables will not as a rule be considered to be instruments in the proper sense, since they are not 'data'. Certain components of these variables are data, however; and sometimes there may be direct government control of prices as well as of wage rates or land rents. A general way of influencing them is to change the *rate of exchange*, probably the most powerful instrument, but an instrument that can only incidentally be used. In addition, this instrument can hardly be said to be an internal instrument.

Whatever the precise instrument chosen, the main point to be made here is again that the regulation of the general price level of a country is an important, and in fact indispensable, element of a country's economic policy. Its economic function is a *regulation*, or adjustment, *of the country's competitive power*. The necessity to adjust may appear from time to time from its general development. If a country can only maintain high and stable employment by permanent inflation this is an indication of the necessity to adjust its competitive power. Of course the better way would be a general increase in its productivity; but this cannot, as a rule, be obtained within a short period. There may be, then, no other way out than a devaluation or a general reduction in prices and income rates.

Of course, the necessity to use this difficult complex of instruments will be the less frequent the smaller the fluctuations in prices in the world's leading countries. The importance of a policy of stable prices in those countries will be clear, therefore (cf. ch. VIII).

VII.5. It may be hoped that an appropriate use of the two groups of main instruments — financial policy and price policy in the above sense — will as a rule lead to a fairly stable development of national income as a whole. An appropriate use presupposes, however, one important condition. *Business men should have and should show understanding for this policy.* They ought not to be alarmed by temporary increases in government activity meant to compensate for their own decreased activity. They seemed to be alarmed in the thirties, especially in the United States, and consequently became reluctant to start investment activity after the 1932 turning point. By so doing they undermined government policy and indirectly national well-being. By such an attitude — if continued *ad absurdum* — any policy, even the best one, may be undermined; it is not constructive. Fortunately there have been profound changes to the good in the understanding shown by business for this type of economic policy.

VII.6. As already observed, the instruments affecting the general level of activity are likely to influence also other countries' well-being, either in the same direction or in the opposite direction as the well-being of the country considered. In the terms previously used they will either be supporting or conflicting instruments and for that reason their decentralized use would probably lead to deviations from the international optimum situation. In periods of depression an increase in expenditure or a decrease in taxes is not only in the interest of the country itself, but also of the other countries. The country concerned might therefore underestimate the advantages and apply the instrument to a lesser degree than desirable. Or, to say it in other terms, *concerted action* may lead to better results than un-co-ordinated action. The risks for the individual country that by an isolated application of these instruments it would adversely affect its balance of payments and hence its gold reserve, may keep such a country from taking action if there is no concerted action. Similar conclusions may be drawn for the opposite case of general inflation where the interest of all countries is concerted action to decrease expenditure.

While expenditures and tax receipts are examples of supporting instruments of national economic policy, man-ipulations of the general price level — either by wage policy or by a policy of changing exchange rates — are of the conflicting type. Lowering the general price level will, as a rule, bring competitive advantages to the country that applies it, at the expense of other countries. Or, in well-known terms, they represent a 'beggar-my-neighbour' policy; in still other terms there is sometimes a danger of a 'competition in devaluation', as in the thirties. For these reasons also these instruments should be subject to inter-national supervision in some form or another (cf. Ch. IX).

Using our own terminology of chapter VI, there is scope therefore to more or less *centralize the use of the instruments just discussed*, with a view to intensify the use of supporting and reduce the use of conflicting instruments. When applying this device we should, however, keep in mind that the character of the same instruments may vary ac-cording to circumstances. If there is not a general depression, but a depression in a few countries, it may be wise to increase expenditure in the depressed group and to decrease it elsewhere; and even if generally speaking we wanted to reduce the use of devaluation as a policy, there may be circumstances in which some country precisely has to devalue.

While advocating a certain central control of the instruments just discussed we keep clearly in mind the strong resistance existing against such a control. It should therefore be confined to the indispensable minimum required by our analysis, which, it should not be forgotten, is based on the aim of the general well-being of the nations as a group and should be accepted for that reason as a strong argument. This indispensable minimum is that the relevant elements for other countries' well-being are (1) the value of the 'inflationary' or 'deflationary gap', i.e. the difference between total expenditure and total income rather than each of these two separately and (2) the general price level of each country. Central control should therefore bear on these two crucial elements and one could leave the choice of the components to the countries themselves. Since the inflationary of deflationary gap of the country as a whole equals the gap in the private sector plus the one in the public sector and the first will only be under indirect control of the government, the primary object for central control should be the 'gap' in the public sector (cf. Ch. XI).

VII.7. Even if a smooth development of national income is warranted, problems may nevertheless remain for *individual industries*. There are continuous changes in technology, in tastes, in natural conditions and occasionally these may suddenly threaten some industries. In the long run this may mean that certain plants will have to vanish and factors of

114

production to move to other industries. In the short run such changes cannot be made without creating grave difficulties. There is a need, therefore, for temporary support to such industries in one form or another. Here the *subsidiary instruments of economic policy* may be useful. They may be *credit policy*, changes in *individual taxes* — to which allusion was already made — or *temporary subventions*. They may even be *temporary import duties*, if these are more easily organized than alternative measures. In special cases where the price mechanism does not work efficiently, quantitative restrictions on imports or on demand generally, or supply or, finally, on both, may even be needed. This is true especially if there are sudden disturbances of equilibrium of some extent in markets where demand and supply are highly inelastic (agricultural markets).

The instruments now under discussion, intended to change the distribution of activity rather than its general level, should be, to a lesser degree, subject to international supervision. Their influence on other countries' well-being is less pronounced and they therefore approach the neutral type of instrument more closely. This device might also be formulated in the following way: relevant to foreign countries and therefore ineligible for decentralization is the total surplus or deficit on public account; much less relevant, however, and hence appropriate for decentralized use is the distribution over the composing items. The irrelevance of this distribution for foreign countries is accentuated by the temporary character recommended for these 'subsidiary' instruments.

Since it is a well-known tendency, however, for such instruments (i.e. taxes, subsidies or quantitative restrictions applied to specific industries) to be used for a longer time than intended originally, it should be emphasized that they anyhow should not hamper, in the long run, the correct use of productive resources from the international point of view. They should be *temporary* only if they, in order to break a shock, do hamper such a correct use and they should, if not conceived of as temporary, obey certain rules to make sure that they do not *invalidate the international division of labour*. An important example is to be found in the system of indirect taxes as handled by most countries. Usually high taxes (excises) on certain commodities like tobacco products, alcoholic beverages and some other luxuries exist. There are provisions, however, that exports of such products are not taxed to the same extent: there are *exemptions* or *draw-backs* tending to neutralize the tax. At the same time there are '*compensatory duties*' on the imports of such products, in order to equalize the burdens on foreign importers and home producers. Such provisions attempt not to falsify the decisions of producers as to what to produce for the international market. The rule should be, indeed, that the tax burden for different products, when exported, should not be different, so as to let relative costs of production reflect the relative real sacrifices necessary to obtain the various products.

CHAPTER VIII

THE INTEGRATION OF CURRENT
TRANSACTIONS

VIII.1. After having discussed certain aspects of national economic policies that are relevant to international relations we are now going to discuss international economic policy, i.e. the handling of *instruments directly affecting international transactions*. In this chapter we will confine ourselves to *non-monetary* instruments and to instruments relevant to the current items on the balances of payments. These items are, as is known, the ones referring to trade and the current transactions of services. Our discussion is devoted to the policies needed to obtain an integration of the current process of production and consumption of a group of free countries, or all free countries; in particular as far as the transactions between nations are involved.

The instruments to be discussed are in particular *quantitative restrictions* (Q.R.) on current transactions and *import duties*. Recent policies of integration, especially in Europe, but also elsewhere, have been primarily concerned with these instruments. On the basis of the main thesis of the free-trade doctrine their *elimination* is considered the main aim of this policy. It should be observed that this is not a complete policy of integration and that it rather represents the *negative part* of such a policy. This is not to deny its importance, however.

VIII.2. As will be clear from the foregoing, and especially from chapter II, this elimination of trade barriers only promises the full results expected from them *if certain preliminary conditions are fulfilled;* in particular, the full use of all productive forces should be warranted. We take it for granted, therefore, that the individual governments follow a policy of high and stable employment, as set out in chapter VII. As a supplement to these national policies, certain international policies, apt to support stability in activity should be adhered to, namely, policies aiming at *price stability.* Although it is probable that price movements are largely a consequence of movements in activity, there are nevertheless certain forces originating from unstable prices which may, as autonomous factors, threaten stability. These forces are of a speculative character: the tendency to accumulate stocks of raw materials in periods of rising prices and to destock during periods of falling prices being the most important; another being the tendency to overestimate profits in times of rising prices and to underrate them when prices fall, which on its turn influences general investment activity. For these reasons the safest foundation for international economic integration would be an international policy of stabilization of raw material prices.[1]

One way of attaining stable raw material prices may be a set of separate *'commodity agreements'*, i.e. agreements on schedules to regulate trade and if necessary stocking and even production of a number of individual commodities. Past history shows that it is not at all a simple matter to obtain and maintain co-operation between the many countries usually involved, with their diverging interests. The question may well be put whether a really satisfactory

---

[1] The safety thus advocated may be compared with the safety habits in technology: it is customary to require standards, in many cases, of two- or threefold safety. This surplus of safety is not considered superfluous.

solution of this problem is not possible only within the framework of a much more powerful centre of international co-operation than has existed so far; indeed, whether a policy of commodity agreements can not be realised only in a world of war economies or a similar world. This is not to say that the present aversion to such agreements is justified.

Another way to attain a stabilized price level of raw materials may be the introduction of a *'raw material standard'* as discussed in chapter IV. By its automatic operation this standard would avoid many of the great difficulties of a set of commodity agreements and show several advantages in stead. In particular it would leave in tact the forces of demand and supply for the separate commodities. On the other hand there would be the possibility, if necessary, to operate schemes for some commodities showing strong disequlibria.

VIII.3. Assuming, then, that national employment policies are such as to guarantee the use of all, or nearly all, productive forces, the optimum *division of labour between nations* will be obtained by free trade with few exceptions. It follows that the best policy in the present circumstances, where for various reasons a number of impediments to trade exist, is the abolition of these obstacles. It consists of two parts, namely the *elimination of quantitative restrictions* or quotas, now called 'liberalization of trade' and the *elimination of import duties*. This elimination cannot be a sudden one. The process of adaptation requires time. Workers have to be re-trained; capital equipment has to be transformed. Without this retraining and this transformation they would be unemployed, i.e. they would not contribute anything to production, which is worse than contributing in a protected industry. The process of elimination should be of the order of length of the minimum period of training, or transformation. Losses of transition would be completely avoided if only new young generations of workers had to be trained for the new industries and if only annual re-investment had to be redirected. But the longer the period of transition, the greater the losses due to a non-optimal division of labour between nations. The process of elimination of Q.R. and tariffs should therefore be of such duration as to make the total loss a minimum. Intuitively, since the complete regular replacement of workers and equipment may take some 20 years, periods of some 10 years have therefore been chosen to represent the most desirable period.

VIII.4. Certain *exceptions* are generally admitted: agricultural production has to be maintained to a certain extent for strategic and for social reasons. Infant industries may be protected temporarily; here mostly a period of five years is taken as acceptable. Nevertheless it may be questioned whether import duties should not always be avoided and *subsidies* be applied where protection is considered legitimate. Subsidies, in particular as a lump sum meant to cover part of an industry's fixed costs, do not affect marginal costs and hence do not 'falsify' prices. They have the political advantage that their payment has to be a deliberate act and cannot be hidden from the public. Only in cases where the administration of subsidies would be more complicated, and hence more costly, than the administration of duties, may the latter be preferred.

VIII.5. The general abolition of import duties by a high-tariff country will affect the competitive position of the country. The general price and wage level of such a country will be higher than that of a low-tariff country. In order to maintain the competitive position, and hence the balance of payments equilibrium, the country has to be permitted to *adjust its exchange rate* accordingly.

VIII.6. There are, in principle, *two ways* of reaching a state without trade impediments. Q.R. and duties may be lowered in all sectors of economy by parallel successive steps; or they may be abolished successively in different sectors. The latter method has been called the method of *partial integration*. Its well-known example is the *European Coal and Steel Community*, where all Q.R. and duties have been eliminated at once between the six countries concerned (Belgium, France, Germany, Italy, Luxembourg and the Netherlands). Clearly the situation created by partial integration is one of disequilibrium. Wages in a high-tariff country will be higher than they could be without tariffs. In the integrated sector production will be less attractive in such a country, tending to reduce the volume of production by more than a correct international division of labour would require. Only after the tariffs in the other sectors also have been eliminated, would equilibrium be restored. If integration of the other sectors is postponed too long, tensions may become too strong: there may be attempts to lower wages in the integrated sector which, from the social point of view, would only be acceptable after the general level of prices (and hence of the cost of living) had become adapted to a general low-tariff situation. Partial integration should be followed as soon as possible, therefore, by integration of other sectors as well, or by general reductions in tariffs.

VIII.7. So far we have only discussed measures of *negative* integration, i.e. policies directed towards the elimination of certain instruments of international economic policy. It is sometimes believed that these are sufficient to obtain the consequences of a better division of labour between nations and a higher standard of life. It may be that these consequences develop automatically; but this will be a slow process which may be accelerated by *positive action*. This positive policy of integration consists of two elements. First, there is a need for certain *supplementary measures* in order to *remove inconsistencies* that may exist between the duties and taxes of different countries. With free trade between a number of countries it is desirable that *duties* and *excises*, e.g. should not be different. Also too great differences in direct taxes may be undesirable, although they are less disturbing than differences in indirect taxes. Certain adjustments will therefore be needed.

Secondly, there is a need for positive action in the field of *production*. The optimum division of labour is a complicated matter, implying reduction of the number of types produced by one plant, specialization of plants on special types and a distribution of the market. Questions about the supply of parts to assembling plants arise, etc. It may be left to the free forces of competition to arrive at a satisfactory situation, but probably it will be a quicker way if such a reorganization program is taken up deliberately and prepared in detail. This does not mean that such action cannot be private. It should be, if possible; but the governments may stimulate it and act if no private action comes about.

VIII.8. The question may be put what the *probable extent* of the improvement in standards of life as a consequence of integration will be. So far little has been done to estimate it. The discussions have been almost entirely qualitative. Nevertheless it seems indispensable for any action that some idea should exist as to what the consequences are likely to be; if only to compare advantages and costs. Detailed studies for separate industries are badly wanted. Some light may be thrown upon this aspect also by macro-economic estimates. The only attempt known to the author has been made by Professor P. J. VERDOORN[1] who confined himself to an estimate of the shifts in trade patterns that may arise as a direct consequence of an elimination of tariffs only. The restriction is twofold: possible consequences of the elimination of Q.R. are disregarded and no attempt is made to estimate the indirect consequences — those working via a change in the organization of production. This latter may be the most important change to be hoped for and hence Prof. Verdoorn's estimates are minima anyhow. Also they do not try to estimate the change in average productivity (and hence real income), but only the shifts in trade. Even so they are interesting. As will be clear, the problem has to be specified much more before even an attempt to solve it can be made. The countries involved, the common tariff they apply to the outside world and the measures they take in order to maintain balance of payments equilibrium have to be specified. In the table below the results have been given for the hypothetical case that the six countries of the Coal and Steel Community were to unite into one customs union, where the tariff applied to other countries equals the average of the tariffs of the six countries and

[1] Welke zijn de achtergronden en vooruitzichten van de economische integratie in Europa en welke gevolgen zou deze integratie hebben, met name voor de welvaart in Nederland? Praeadvies 1952 voor de Vereniging voor de Staathuishoudkunde.

TRADE AND ITS PRESUMABLE CHANGES AS A CONSEQUEN

COAL AND STEEL COMMUNIT

(Figures for 1951; finished products only;

Importing countries	Expo		
	Netherlands	*B.L.E.U.*	*France*
Netherlands		363 (— 8)	73 (+
B.L.E.U.	186 (— 4)		174 (+
France	71 (+11)	167 (+20)	
W. Germany	198 (+33)	118 (+15)	151 (+
Italy	25 (+ 6)	48 (+ 4)	69 (+
All Schuman-countries together	480 (+46)	696 (+31)	467 (+
Rest of the world	986 (—82)	1170 (—71)	2472 (—
Total exports	1466 (—36)	1866 (—40)	2939 (+

where balance of payments equilibrium is obtained by an adaptation of exchange rates. The changes in trade estimated by Prof. Verdoorn on the basis of a number of hypotheses as to elasticities of demand and supply, are given in brackets, whereas the trade pattern for 1951 is given for reference (cf. table VIII).

A CUSTOMS UNION BETWEEN THE COUNTRIES OF THE
MILLIONS OF $

umptions made see text and original publication.)

tries

*. Germany	Italy	All Schuman-countries together	Rest of the world	Total imports
4 (+31)	28 (+ 6)	708 (+43)	615 (—32)	1323 (+11)
5 (+17)	27 (+ 5)	552 (+44)	477 (—36)	1029 (+ 8)
4 (+21)	114 (+24)	586 (+76)	1334 (—14)	1920 (+62)
	114 (+24)	581 (+97)	786 (—43)	1367 (+54)
6 (+16)		268 (+39)	546 (+11)	814 (+50)
9 (+85)	283 (+59)	2695 (+299)	3758 (—114)	6453 (+185)
9 (—82)	1062 (—22)	7549 (—285)		7549 (—285)
8 (+ 3)	1345 (+37)	10244 (+14)	3758 (—114)	14002 (—100)

CHAPTER IX

MONETARY INTEGRATION

IX.I. After having discussed the use to be made of the instruments of economic policy that directly influence, as such, current transactions between nations, we will now deal with the *monetary instruments*, i.e. with the techniques of international payments and their integration. From the nature of things and their treatment in the analytical chapters it will be clear that current transactions may as well be directly influenced by any regulations of their payments; transactions that cannot be paid for having little chance to be repeated. The central question behind this theme is of course, what organization of international payments deserves preference. From Chapter V in particular it will be clear that this organization has to depend on the fulfilment of certain equilibrium conditions, without which a payments system cannot work. We will come back to these conditions after a while.

Assuming that they are fulfilled it is clear that the simplest and therefore theoretically best organization of international payments would be the introduction of a *world currency*, a very appealing idea, much also to the layman. With a world currency no transformation of one type of money into another would be necessary and all the trouble connected with it — changes in exchange rates and their risks, inconvertibility — could be avoided, it seems. It is often forgotten that such a world currency could only work if certain rather rigorous conditions of 'good behaviour' are fulfilled (which some people think they could get rid of under a world currency) and that if these conditions are fulfilled, a system of convertible national currencies would work smoothly just as well. The main condition is that there should be monetary equilibrium for each separate area, i.e. equality between income and expenditure, as far as such an area would not receive deliberate 'help' from others or would have reserves at its disposal. For the word 'area' we could also read, in this connection, 'group of families', or 'group of enterprises', or finally, 'one family' or 'one enterprise'. A world currency, in other words, would not help any individual or any group to overcome a deficit in his or its finance, if nobody was inclined to help.

In a way this would therefore be a rigorous means to enforce monetary equilibrium on those who have no reserves; but this is the very reason why most national governments would not like to hand over their sovereign rights to create money; they want to be free to make deficits if their policy implies such deficits. Only if there would be complete political homogeneity between the national governments and the central financial authority, could no difficulties arise. This implies that agreement could be obtained, at any time, on the extra help that certain governments should receive or on the amounts some governments would have to make available to others. The necessary prerequisite therefore would be that there be political unity already: that the machinery to deal with such questions existed and worked sufficiently smoothly.

Apart from these conditions it is doubtful whether in a world *threatened by wars* even the set of allied countries could permit itself the 'luxury' of one common currency. Such a currency would be upset by any more general attempt at capital flight, say from threatened areas. No new investments would perhaps be made at all in such areas if the world currency system made it possible to use savings for investment in remote parts of the world without any permission. Some distribution in 'watertight' compartments as far as capital movements are concerned would seem indispensable.

IX.2. If, on the other hand, for current transactions and the permissible capital transactions taken together, the condition of monetary equilibrium is fulfilled, a system of national currencies can yield without much trouble almost the same services as are expected from a world currency. There may be convertibility for these transactions and hence no hindrance of normal intercourse.

It cannot be denied, however, that then the problem of *changes in exchange rates* does remain; a problem with several aspects. On the one hand the possibility to change rates gives an opportunity to regulate the price level of separate countries in order to adapt their competitive position to changed conditions. On the other hand it means the existence of certain risks for trade, especially if the changes can be large. It is not easy to construct a system without any drawbacks. The system of *flexible exchange rates* has the advantage of smooth and hence small changes, but the disadvantage of speculative deviations which it is difficult to eliminate completely and the disadvantage of arbitrariness in short-term policy. During the later depression years of the thirties it was advocated under the impression of the wide price movements which it was hoped would be avoided by changes in exchange rates. Upon closer consideration and in the hypothesis of a better anti-cyclic policy experts have since the war generally turned towards a system of fixed rates which would only need incidental adaptations; and this has been made the basis of the International Monetary Fund.

IX.3. Since, in our terminology, changes in exchange rates are conflicting instruments of economic policy, they should be under some control of an international agency, and their use should be restricted. Such is the theory of the Bretton Woods Agreement on which the International Monetary Fund is based. The practice so far has been that not very much 'control' has been possible. There is of course some hesitation to use the instrument, since devaluation will hardly be considered a glorious performance of the country applying it, but when applied it is almost autonomously applied. Perhaps the only conceivable brake on too frequent and too big changes could be a set of sanctions in the field of credits.

A prerequisite of a minimum of changes in rates is, as was already observed, equilibrium in the balances of payments. Apart from a complete regulation of all trans-actions — not very attractive to Western countries — this will, in the short run, only be possible if sufficient reserves are available. These may partly be centralized in an inter-national 'equalization fund' such as the International Monetary Fund.

In the long run equilibrium can only be maintained if, as was set out in Chapter VII, national economic policy is one of monetary equilibrium at a high level of employment. This not only implies a certain financial policy, directed towards monetary equilibrium, but at the same time a certain *price and wage policy*, directed towards the mainte-nance of competitive power. Only with such a price and wage policy will it be conceivable to avoid changes in ex-change rates. In many countries recent trends have been towards a great rigidity in wages and prices, as a consequence of increased organization of the labour market and of the markets of many industrial and agricultural products. Adaptability is further hampered by cost-of-living clauses in labour contracts and similar attempts to maintain the purchasing power of incomes under all circumstances. The question may be put whether this is, in the end, a desirable policy. Experience in the Netherlands gives some courage to those who believe that an improved understanding of the functioning of the economy from trade unions and employers' unions may make it possible to reduce price and wage rigidity. The workers should be also confident that if adjustments are necessary they will be applied to all groups in an equitable way. Such confidence can only exist if there are certain standards of decency in economic negotiations, together with a well-balanced political system in which all groups of the population participate. Without such possibilities to reduce price and wage rigidity there will be no chance, apart from adjustments in capital movements, to avoid adjustments in exchange rates.

IX.4. *Capital movements*, in fact, may have an important equilibrating function. *Short-term* capital movements were already implied, to some extent, when we spoke of the functions of reserves and of an international equalization fund. Private short-term capital movements will be possible as far as trade credits can be somewhat adapted to the situation. The other types of private short-term capital movements, which played an important role in the quiet periods of the nineteenth century, are generally considered less helpful in a world where fresh disturbances may come up for political reasons. They may, then, take the form of 'hot money', moving nervously from one financial centre to the other and often doing more harm than good. In the present time of restricted freedom of capital movements they have been more or less eliminated and, therefore, are not able, on the other hand, to exert any equilibrating force either.

Long-term capital movements remain, both private and public. Although these usually will have another primary object they nevertheless do or can also have a function in the maintenance of equilibrium in the balance of payments. It is only natural that countries with a surplus of capital formation supply capital to countries with a deficit in capital formation. By a surplus of capital formation we mean a surplus in relation to the investments that should be made at home, judged from an international economic point of view, taken in the widest sense. If for political or psychological reasons, say fear of war risks, such a capital transfer does not take place in the private sphere, there may be scope for public action. Some of the well-known disequilibria of the post-war time ('dollar scarcity'; or the Italian balance of payments) may in this way be remedied to some extent.

In order that capital movements be an equilibrating and not a disequilibrating factor, certain conditions have also to be fulfilled regarding the distribution of a country's assets and liabilities over the various *'degrees of liquidity'*. The amounts due for amortization should correspond to the amounts available every period of time. Difficult situations have sometimes arisen because of lack of such correspondence. Germany in 1931 had short-term debts against illiquid assets. The 'sterling balances' accumulated during World War II in a number of countries of the Commonwealth should, from the debtor's standpoint, have been long-term debts, since there was no possibility for

Britain to pay them off in a short period. There was a tendency with the creditor countries, however, to spend part of the balance in a short time, especially as far as they wanted to apply them for reconstruction purposes. This lack of correspondence has to be removed before sterling can be made convertible, either by a change in the status of the balances or by compensatory provisions such as foreign loans.

IX.5. The Second World War caused heavy *disturbances in financial equilibria* that have, so far, only been partly over-come. Perhaps the most important single disturbance was caused by financing war expenditure by Great Britain — just referred to — which made it necessary for that country to sell considerable amounts of foreign investments and to incur important debts with some countries of the Common-wealth, notably Egypt, India and Australia. These debts, already referred to above, amounted to some 3½ to 4 milliards of sterling at the end of 1945. The sale of assets implied an important loss of interest and dividend income to the United Kingdom, throwing the current balance of payments out of equilibrium.

In large parts of the world current items of the balances of payments were equally thrown out of equilibrium as a consequence of deficit financing, itself a consequence of decreased productivity, increased needs and the presence of abundant means of payments. From the international point of view this deficit financing could, of course, only go on as long as the countries concerned were prepared to exhaust their gold reserves and as long as foreign govern-ments were prepared to supply credits or grants, but the pressing character of the needs accumulated during the war created that preparedness. Since it was felt that foreign currency should not be spent on luxuries or semi-luxuries, trade and payment were subjected to numerous restrictions. As far as these restrictions were of a monetary character, their aim was to impose economy on the use of hard currencies, in particular on the use of dollars. In 1947 a first attempt was made at restoring, by decree, the convertibility of sterling into dollars. In order to break the first shock a loan of about $4 milliard was accorded by the United States to the United Kingdom. Nevertheless the operation was not successful. Demand for dollars so much surpassed supply of them that the loan was exhausted very rapidly and monetary restrictions had to be re-established.

IX.6. With the gradual improvement of productivity and the aid supplied by the *Marshall Plan* (or European Recovery Plan, ERP), adding up to about $ 20 milliard, in a period of about 4 years, the European countries, united in the Organization for European Economic Cooperation (OEEC), were able to restore mutual convertibility in 1950. This was effected by the establishment of the European Payments Union (EPU), prolonged in 1952 and 1954, which introduced a system of inter-European clearing of current payments. Deficits of a member country A with respect to another member country B could be financed with surpluses with regard to some third member country C. Countries showing a deficit with the group as a whole received credits in EPU units up to a certain amount: beyond that limit they partly received credits and partly had to pay in gold. The proportion of gold increased as the cumulated deficit grew and beyond a further limit no further credits were granted. Creditor countries, on the other hand, had to give credit to the EPU up to a certain amount, then would receive an increasing proportion in gold. The group could not operate without some external aid, however; an initial reserve was granted by the United States, which was later increased. Nevertheless, by 1954 the position of the group as a whole was very near to equilibrium. Convertibility for current items with regard to the dollar for a number of European countries would seem possible at the moment of writing (summer 1954).

Re-establishment of such convertibility for the stronger among the European countries would, as we have seen in Chapter V, bring some of the weaker countries in a more difficult position and some provisions would have to be made in order to help them solve their problems. Looking at the world at large, outside Europe, a number of under-developed countries remains with more or less serious balance of payments problems, especially in Latin America. A general system of convertibility throughout the non-communist world, at least as far as current items on the balances of payments are concerned would have to be based on three main elements. First, a programme of capital transfers based on a comprehensive scheme of development programmes should be drawn up; (b) the strong countries should effectuate further reductions in tariffs with a view to develop world trade and (c) thirdly, the weaker countries should follow more orthodox financial policies which might be facilitated by the first and second parts of the programme.

The process towards convertibility has to be in line with the process towards the realisation of free trade. A country, or group of countries, in process of revalidation will, at any moment during that process, have a certain degree of 'hardness', which only gradually increases. It may use this hardness in either of two ways; it may either increase the convertibility of its currency or it may increase the degree of liberalization in its trade. It can, however, only permit itself more convertibility at the cost of less freedom in trade, or more freedom in trade at the cost of less convertibility. The best way to use its degree of hardness so far attained is to have a certain harmony between these two virtues; and only if the 'hardness' reached is complete will it be possible to restore completely both convertibility and freedom.

CHAPTER X

THE INTEGRATION OF DEVELOPMENT

x.1. So far international economic policy has been discussed on the basis of a given distribution of resources, i.e. land and capital, over nations. As was discussed already in chapter I, this distribution is far from satisfactory, however: it is extremely uneven if calculated per head of population. This unevenness is partly due to artificial impediments to the movement of the factors of production, especially to the movement of population. For another portion it is probably due to differences in mental attitude and abilities between nations. However that may be, the extreme inequality is becoming a source of important future tensions. Traffic has increased, as have communications generally; people are more and more becoming conscious of the great differences and less and less prepared to take them for granted. They are helped in this attitude by communist propaganda. A complication is the increasing rather than decreasing divergency of standards of life: whereas some young countries among the underdeveloped are struggling with the problems set by their newly obtained independency and thereby are stagnating in economic development, the leading developed countries are increasing production even more rapidly than before. This divergency in standards of life threatens political unity in the non-communist world, in the world at large as well as inside Europe.

x.2. It has been believed that there are automatic forces at work towards an equalization of welfare. One of the well-known arguments is that of the so-called 'factor price equalization'. The argument says that specialization of wealthy countries on capital-intensive industries and of poorer countries on labour-intensive industries will make it possible to pay the same wage rate and the same interest rate in both types of countries. This specialization, it is maintained, only requires free trade in final products which might take the place of movements of population or capital. This argument has only limited validity, as has been shown by further research. It is not of a general validity and depends on the figures involved. If the differences in capital intensity between industries are smaller than the differences between countries the equalization of wages and interest is not possible. What is also relevant in this context is that some of the more capital-intensive industries produce products that cannot be transported at all and have to be produced inside each country (electricity, traffic services, 'dwelling services').

An even greater difficulty arises if the capital intensities of the various conceivable industries are each of them higher than the capital intensity of the country (i.e. the ratio of the quantity of capital available to the quantity of labour). In such a case (cf. also section 11.5) not even all labour can be employed for lack of capital. In such a situation we may speak of an '*absolute scarcity of capital*'.

It may be safely stated that as long as factors are not permitted to move much more freely than today, not very much can be hoped for an equalization of wages and interest rates or even for a full employment of labour. The only solution for the problem of diverging standards of life is in a more intensive movement of factors. Essentially, what is needed is the integration of the process of development; the growth of a country should not be considered a problem only regarding that one country and to be accomplished practically with the country's own investments. It is part of a world problem of equilibrated growth. In this connection it should be recognized that the problem is partly one of population policy. If populations in the poorer countries had increased less rapidly, their welfare would certainly have been higher. One indispensable element of the solution consists of the recognition of this fact and the willingness to apply what the Indian government calls 'family planning'.

x.3. In some quarters it has been believed that the standards of life of the poorer countries could be raised, so to say, by decree. It was believed that prescription of higher wages and equalization of labour conditions generally, would be a road towards eliminating 'social dumping'. This is a misunderstanding of the economic forces at work. The main effect of such measures will be to reduce the number of workers that can at all be employed in such countries. Higher standards of life can, for the populations as a whole, only be obtained out of direct aid or out of increases in production. A considerable rise in production can only be obtained by considerable increases in capital invested, training and by spreading of technical knowledge. Direct aid for an enormous population such as in a country like India would have to be so large, if the remedy had to come from such aid, that it would be out of the question. Whatever contributions can be obtained should be used for investment as far as possible and even then very considerable amounts would be needed (cf. x.4). The investments needed most are of the 'basic' type, i.e. for the improvement of the productive basis of the country: land improvement, irrigation, supply of energy, improvement of the transport system and of education and housing. Many of these investments are hardly remunerative in the private sense of the word. But they appear to be the decisive element which makes industrialized countries attractive to further investment. Once they are there, all production is easier.

It is virtually impossible to increase capital formation inside the underdeveloped countries in any way sufficient to meet the demands which only a modest development would put to it. The reason is the low average income in the countries, of which little can be saved. This is a self-evident phenomenon observable inside every developed country also: the poor do not save. Only the high incomes could and do save; but their numbers are very small in these countries. Of course no attempt should be neglected to increase savings; but it would not be realistic to expect much from this source.

x.4. If the serious problem we are discussing is to be treated at all seriously there should at least be an attempt at programming, for the next five to ten years, what would seem to be a reasonable target. We are only at the very beginning of such programming. Inside the countries, programmes of investment are being executed on the basis of the present resources. In the international agencies whose task is nearest to the task we have in mind, a series of studies have now been made as to the capital requirements needed under various assumptions. An attempt at choosing a definite programme among the alternatives presented has not been made and still less an attempt at procuring the means needed. The responsibility is not yet clearly recognized by the agencies of economic co-operation so far in existence and lacking this recognition, there is more decentralization than seems appropriate. The attempts made so far at estimating the capitals needed under the assumptions of putting a halt to the divergency of standards of life do show anyhow that these capitals are very considerable. The estimates for total investment needed range from $10 to $15 milliards annually, of which some $5 milliards are supplied by the countries themselves and some $2 milliards by the various agencies which are in operation. There would be a gap of $3 to $8 milliards per annum. This is a few per cent of the combined incomes of the developed countries: nevertheless it is a very considerable amount.

There is little prospect that the missing amounts can ever be invested by private investors. Political uncertainty is a first handicap; the unwillingness of many underdeveloped countries to admit private enterprises from the developed countries, unfounded though it may be, another. Perhaps the most important factor is, however, that many of the most urgent investments would not be of the self-liquidating type. All these considerations point to the desirability of new methods of financing, of which the most open form would be the establishment of an '*international investment budget*'. Public opinion will have to get accustomed to the idea that these sums will simply have to be supplied as grants, in the common interest of all concerned.

The establishment of a common investment budget creates huge problems of various kinds: political and administrative. The first basic principle should be that the sums involved should be used efficiently and this raises all sorts of questions concerning the standards of efficiency in different countries and the ways to avoid national sensitivities.

The second basic principle should be that the contributions to it should be equal for persons of equal real incomes in the various countries.

These two principles would, when adhered to, at the same time be the most powerful and direct means to educate public opinion in the basic concepts of international co-operation and responsibility. On the one hand people would be reminded permanently and personally of some of the main tasks of the international community, and, on the other hand, they would get accustomed to being treated individually according to one and the same international standard of taxation. The institution of the common international budget would, it may be added, be a logical continuation of a similar process of centralization inside many of the member countries.

CHAPTER XI

THE AGENCIES OF INTERNATIONAL ECONOMIC CO-OPERATION

XI.1. In the preceding chapters a system of international economic policy directed towards integration was described. The degree of centralization needed for the execution of the corresponding tasks was also discussed. We will now discuss what agencies will have to be charged with these tasks: to what extent will the existing national agencies be able to perform them, to what extent will they have to be switched over to existing international agencies or have they already been switched over? To what extent, finally, will there be a need for new international agencies? This problem of the organization of international economic policy is ultimately connected with the problem of political integration, which may be said to represent also a problem of 'optimum centralization'. A politically integrated area is the ideal area for the application of an integrated economic policy and vice versa; the two aspects can hardly be divorced. In this respect it is useful to distinguish between the integration of the economies and the integration of economic policy itself. An integrated economic policy presupposes the existence of a 'common policy' or a 'harmonized policy'; and part of the integration process therefore consists of a discussion between partners, which policy they are able to follow all of them. The common policy has to be, by necessity, a compromise; the best compromise will be one which can be based on certain scientific principles of consistency. Even then, of course, the common policy may be less interventionist or more interventionist, according to the prevailing tastes in this respect, and according to the circumstances. In times of serious disequilibria a more interventionist policy could be preferred than in times of equilibrium.

There are, unfortunately, many discrepancies between the composing elements of which the ideal degree of co-operation was assumed for a while. The peoples — or only the governments, or both — may not be prepared yet to co-operate to the extent which might be desirable for purely economic reasons. They also may not be prepared to co-operate to the extent to which their own long-term interest would seem to require political integration. In all such circumstances other solutions than the optimal ones will have to be accepted, if only temporary or as a first step. And we should not exclude the possibility that experience about co-operation would in the end have to teach something to all concerned, also to the advocates of integration. Instead of a central organ for a certain function, only a co-ordination of the policies of decentralized organs, or only consultations in particular circumstances may be chosen. Our discussion in this chapter will be based on the assumption that the desire for co-operation exists; it may accordingly sometimes be biassed in order to contribute to further development.

Tasks of local or national interest only should of course be left to local or national organs: this is a generally accepted democratic principle. As was set out in chapters VI–X, it is primarily where one government may adversely or favourably affect the interests of other nations that a central agency will be needed. And it is conceivable that certain agencies should be regional in the sense of embracing a group of neighbouring countries only instead of all countries concerned. As far as an agency would have a task with regard to a 'conflicting' instrument of economic policy (the first case just mentioned), its task may primarily be a supervising one; in this case, as we set out previously, the abolition of the use of the instrument may be the best form of centralization, which requires supervision. In the second case, the one of a supporting instrument, a more active task may be needed. Since many instruments may alternatively be conflicting and supporting, both tasks have often to be envisaged. Agencies should be created, as is implied in the foregoing remarks, according to the instruments of economic policy rather than to the aims of that policy. Each instrument will have to be handled with a view to its contribution to all the targets of policy; and each target will have to be attained with the help of several instruments. If there were an agency for each target, an enormous confusion would be created as to who would have to decide on the use of a certain instrument. It is correct therefore that there are agencies supervising tariffs or exchange rates, being instruments. It would not be correct to have an agency dealing with employment policy, which is a target; instead there should be agencies which decide upon public expenditures, taxes, etc. which may be the instruments of economic policy. The agency dealing with expenditures would have, however, to base its decisions not only on the employment target, but on other targets as well. Even then every target could be taken care of provided the number of targets does not surpass the number of instruments.

Instruments and agencies may finally be subdivided into general and partial ones: the general ones having to do with economies as a whole and the partial ones with certain sectors only, as e.g. coal and steel production. It will be clear that the well-being of the sectors may depend to a very high degree on the handling of general instruments. Partial agencies may have a vital interest therefore in the creation of certain general agencies which handle instruments of importance to them.

From our survey of economic policy in chapters VII–X it has become clear that general agencies will be needed in particular for:

1) the supervision and reduction of trade restrictions;
2) the regulation of raw material markets;
3) the supervision of the convertibility of currencies;
4) the supervision of monetary equilibrium and employment policy;
5) the supply of capital for development and
6) the regulation of migration.

In principle, all these tasks should be performed on a world basis, although some may also be subjected to co-operation on a regional basis, under supervision on a world level. In view of the unhappy controversy between the communist and the non-communist countries the co-operation between only a restricted number of countries may prove possible. Regional integration may be useful, if certain instruments of economic policy are only used by a regional group of countries: this may be so either because other countries prefer not to use them or are not able to use them. A condition that must be fulfilled is of course that the nature of the problem to be solved be also regional and not world-wide. Regional regulation of a market with world-wide competition e.g. would not be possible.

In principle agencies have been created by the United Nations for each of the six main tasks indicated; but various difficulties have been encountered.

XI.2. *The supervision and reduction of trade restrictions* should have been the task of the *International Trade Organization* (ITO), which has not, however, come into existence, despite extensive preparatory work; mainly because of the reluctance of the United States to accept the amended charter. Although the tasks with regard to trade restrictions have been taken over by the *General Agreement on Trade and Tariffs* (GATT) it cannot be said that the process of reduction of restrictions has been very successful. This applies both to quantitative restrictions and tariffs. Two main factors are reponsable for these difficulties: (i) the unwillingness of many countries to go faster into the direction of free trade and (ii) the extremely complicated technique adopted to negotiate reductions in tariffs. The common root to both causes is the divergency of interests connected with the existence of tariffs. There is a tendency therefore to maintain certain tariffs of vital importance to some industry and a reluctance, on the part of governments, to accept simple general schemes of reduction of tariffs. Lack of determination and of a somewhat broader outlook on these problems remains another handicap to integration.

In Europe the OEEC has been fairly successful in reducing quantitative restrictions between member countries. In many countries more than 90 per cent of imports is 'liberalized', as the abolition of Q.R. is called. The gains have not been permanent, however, in certain cases, where new difficulties in the general financial position and consequent balance of payments difficulties have led to 'deliberalization'. These experiences, especially in the case of France, point to the necessity of more co-ordination in the field of financial policy. This co-ordination might well be organized in a separate agency (cf. section XI.5.) instead of in ITO itself, as was originally intended; the same may be said with regard to 'commodity agreements' (cf. section XI.3.); and consequently a more permanent organization with largely the same tasks as GATT would then be sufficient. Still it would be desirable if other, and more efficient, methods of reduction of tariffs were adopted.

XI.3. The *regulation of raw material markets* is in principle entrusted to the *Food and Agricultural Organization* (FAO), as far as agricultural products are concerned, and to some more partial and some more temporary organizations, like the *European Coal and Steel Community*, the *Wheat Agreement*, the *International Tin Study Group* and others, for separate commodities and the *Raw Materials Conference* created after the Korean crisis. It is too early yet to judge the results that have been and may in the future be reached by the European Coal and Steel Community. Its problems are more regional anyhow. A considerable degree of success has been obtained with the Wheat Agreement which succeeded in keeping prices of wheat at a stable and moderate level since 1949. The activities with regard to raw materials generally have not been too promising. It has not been possible to avoid the 'Korean boom' in their prices and the subsequent fall. During negotiations on separate raw materials too restricted viewpoints — mostly those in the direct national interest of the negotiators — have been prevailing. Various reports by experts invited by the Secretary-General of the United Nations, stress the desirability of a stabler price level of raw materials. This applies both to the reports on cyclical fluctuations in general and to the report on this subject in particular. With the existing machinery of organizations much more could have been attained if the governments had been prepared to commit themselves to bolder projects.

The question may, however, be repeated (cf. section IV.7.) whether not a much simpler solution of some of the most important aspects involved could be reached by the creation of a 'raw material standard', i.e. the acceptance by some central banks, at a fixed price, of raw material bonds as a monetary reserve. These bonds, as has been set out, would have to represent the property of a 'basket of raw materials' of a fixed composition. The reader may be referred to the section just quoted for further explanations.

XI.4. The *supervision of the convertibility of currencies* and a number of related tasks are the tasks of the *International Monetary Fund* (IMF) which represents an international reserve bank, though with only limited competence and very limited means. Among the international institutions created by the United Nations the Fund is no doubt the best prepared and the best equipped, qualitatively speaking. The organization is staffed with a large number of the best experts, supplies an excellent documentation and its analytical reports (both published and unpublished) are of very high quality. As has repeatedly been emphasized by experts, however, the competence and means at the disposal of the IMF are, however, much too restricted. One group of experts, reporting to the U.N. Secretary-General, contrasted the Funds reserve of about $3 milliards with the temporary need of dollars that might arise in a moderate depression which they estimate at $10 milliards. These experts therefore rightly advocated an increase in the quota to supply by the member countries and a more liberal use of the means.

As long as most of the relatively strong European currencies were not even convertible into dollars there was scope for such regional organizations as the *European Payments Union* (EPU) which constituted convertibility between those European currencies (for current payments) and introduced an automatic system of short-term credits to members. Also here the problem of the extent of available reserves was one of the most important to be faced.

In a way the payments system of the *Sterling Area* yielded similar services to a large member of countries inside and outside the British Empire. Even if, gradually, the point seems to be reached where a restricted convertibility of sterling and of a number of continental European currencies becomes possible, the need for some credit facilities to the remaining inconvertible countries is evident and it may be hoped that somewhat wider competences will be given to the IMF to this effect. As set out before, however, the solution of the convertibility problem has to be found in a combination with long-term capital transfers and with internal measures by a number of the countries concerned.

XI.5. *The supervision of monetary equilibrium and employment policy* is less clearly the task of an existing agency. Annual discussions are now being held in the *Economic and Social Council* (Ecosoc) of the United Nations, on the basis of extensive reports asked from the governments. Although such a discussion in public may certainly have some positive influence on the governments that may be 'in default', there is no direct competence of any institute to give directives to the governments concerned. This seems to be too weak a construction for such an important aspect of economic policy.

A similar situation prevails at the European level. There have been discussions on the internal and the external financial stability of the co-operating countries; and in case a country shows either an accumulated deficit or a surplus of a certain size in EPU, it will have to explain its policy to the other members. Such an explanation will be required especially if the country considers import restrictions in connection with its balance of payments situation. These explanations and the directives that have been emitted to some countries have not, however, led to a clear employment policy on a European level. Even the financial policy in the more restricted sense of maintaining balance of payments equilibrium is only loosely co-ordinated. More specifically, the problem of structural unemployment has not been the subject of any serious attempt to co-operate at an inter-European level.

XI.6. In the field of monetary equilibrium and employment policy, our hint that agencies should be constituted according to the instruments of economic policy they should handle seems to have some special scope. In fact, more than one instrument is involved and their handling should perhaps be separated. On the other hand, the instruments involved are not only important to the realization of monetary equilibrium, but also to the long-term aspects of employment, and to welfare generally, i.e. what is usually summarized as 'development'. When we consider some of these instruments a little more closely, we have to keep this interconnection in mind.

The most powerful instrument in maintaining monetary equilibrium as well as in regulating employment is evidently *public finance*. Our analysis has shown the necessity for international integration also in this field. An agency supervising the main features of public finance, with the power to prescribe their inflationary or deflationary gap would seem the minimum which from the purely economic view-point would be desirable. Only as far as political preparedness to co-operation would fall short of this requirement, less centralized methods, such as consultations, should be attempted.

A 'power to prescribe' a certain deficit or surplus could only be established as far as certain sanctions were introduced as the same time. Such sanctions could be of a twofold nature: they could be the exclusion from credit facilities for the weaker countries and the non-participation in certain international projects of investment for the stronger countries. A strong country that would not co-operate in the desired way might be excluded from participation, or given a smaller share, in the physical execution of some international projects.

A powerful instrument in financial integration would no doubt be the existence of a *common budget*. Participation in the common budget could itself already be adapted to whatever requirements of a monetary character could be made: a country in a state of deflation could be permitted a deficit whereas a country in an inflationary state could be required to have a surplus in the common budget. The expenditure side of the common budget would open the opportunity to increase or decrease any country's participation in international projects just quoted.

XI.7. The task of *supplying capital for development* pertains to the *International Bank for Reconstruction and Development* (IBRD), or 'World Bank'. The insufficiency of this supply has been discussed widely in recent years, even if account is taken of the partial schemes auch as the *Colombo Plan* for the British Empire and some adjacent territories, the *Technical Assistance* of the U.N., the *Point Four* program of the U.S. government and some others. The limitations to the Bank are qualitative as well as quantitative; the financial aid supplied consists of loans, and the resources of the Bank have to be found, apart from the Bank's own restricted capital, in the open capital market. Another U.N. agency has therefore been envisaged, the Special United Nations Fund for Economic Development (SUNFED), which would be able to supply grants. The budget so far proposed would amount to only $\frac{1}{4}$ milliards of dollars, which is small in comparison to the capital needed if development of the underdeveloped countries is to be stimulated sufficiently to overcome the prevailing divergency in living conditions (cf. section x.1.). Here also therefore the idea of the Common Budget would seem to be a natural one, able to co-ordinate the policies in this field much more forcefully. Part of the activities would have to be directed towards increasing the supply of technically skilled staff of which the deficiency is one of the major bottlenecks in development at the present time.

Also at the European level a separate agency for financing development has repeatedly been proposed. For a solution of the problems of Southern Italy in particular such an institution would be of much importance. The case may well be considered a test case for European unity.

An international *regulation of migration* seems even more difficult to realise than the activities already mentioned. With respect to migration the international situation is utterly unsatisfactory: international co-operation squarely broke down several times. Perhaps the biggest single cause of this lack of success is the fast increase in population in the underdeveloped countries; some form of 'family planning' will be indispensable, in the interest of all concerned. Difficult problems will have to be solved, but a dogmatic attitude will not contribute to any solution. A broad view and an open mind will be necessary for all spiritual leaders concerned. Once the problem of population control has been recognized, the regulation of migration will be the smaller task.

xi.8. If we try to summarize our findings and to draw some broad conclusions on the agencies of international economic integration, we may say that important starts have been made. The existing international agencies are nuclei of co-operation around which the agencies needed for the future must 'crystallize'. But they are too small, grown somewhat haphazardly, with only little of the co-ordination our analysis would suggest to be necessary. Even so they already represent an impressive piece of activity, the purely technical difficulties of which are already only too easily underestimated by the general public. If we have criticized their results, this does not mean that their restricted success is their own fault. For the overwhelming part the fault lies with others. In many cases it is not the international 'machinery' which is lacking, but it is the preparedness of governments to use it in the appropriate way. In the larger part of international negotiations it is the short-term or direct national interests which are taken as a criterion rather than the long-term and indirect interest, or international interests as such. It will be difficult for representatives of national governments to diverge very much from these narrower interests because institutionally they are forced to stick to them. The cause for so little progress often is the very existence of national governments. To some extent therefore public opinion and its political expression in the parties will have to take the initiative and will have to enforce the institution of international parliamentary and governmental agencies. Because of the technical complexity of any such activities it will often be necessary for national governments and administrations, who are the best-equipped institutions, to do the jobs, but they can only do so if they have the strong support of public opinion. Two centres of action would seem the most promising, therefore, namely such broad-minded individual initiatives from government quarters as led to the Marshall Plan, the Colombo Plan or the Schuman Plan on the one hand, and initiatives by political parties and ad hoc organizations to educate public opinion on the other hand. Both should base themselves at least partly on such scientific analysis of the problems as attempted in this volume, an analysis, it is hoped, which helps to see which instruments of economic policy are most in need of centralization.

Our analysis on this point has confirmed many view-points which at present govern the endeavours to integration made at the European level as well as, less clearly, at the world level. They have confirmed the desirability of a reduction in quantitative restrictions and in import duties; the desirability of a positive integration of production, of a certain unification of indirect taxes, of convertibility of currencies and of an international policy of development. They have also confirmed that for functions of a more local or national character decentralization would seem desirable. In addition to all this the further conclusion has been reached that an essential element of integration will also have to be a higher degree of centralization in financial policy. This latter conclusion seems to be in accordance with what a long debate on internal economic policy has also taught, namely that with more centralization in financial policy many other instruments of economic policy can be left decentralized.

LITERATURE

The purpose of this list is a very restricted one: to indicate a few titles to those of the readers who want to have an 'entrance' to modern economic literature in the fields touched in this text. Each of the publications mentioned contains further literature. The titles are followed by a brief characteristic for the reader's orientation.

American Economic Association (H. S. ELLIS and L. A. METZLER ed.), Readings in the Theory of International Trade, London 1950 (1953) (collection of some of the best scientific papers published during the last 20 years on the most important problems in the field of theory).

R. F. HARROD, International Economics, Cambridge 1933 (1947) (brief text on theory of international trade for students of economics).

J. E. MEADE, The Balance of Payments, London 1951 (elaborate text, in simple language, on the international aspects of economic policy).

J. E. MEADE, Problems of Economic Union, London 1953 (brief discussion, without mathematics, of fundamental questions of integration).

G. MYRDAL, Toward a More Closely Integrated Free-World Economy (Columbia University Bicentennial) (to be published). (Economic, political and sociological discussion of present state of integration policies.)

G. HABERLER, Currency Convertibility, New York/ Washington 1954 (brief text on one of the topics of the day).

OEEC, Europe, The Way Ahead, Paris 1952 (example of 'progress report' by one of the centres of integration).

In addition the following reports by experts invited by the
U.N. Secretary-General may be recommended:

1. National and international measures for full employment; report by a group of experts appointed by the
   Secretary-General, Lake Success (United Nations,
   Dep. of econ. affairs) 1949.
2. Measures for international economic stability; report
   by a group of experts. New York (United Nations, Dep.
   of econ. affairs) 1951.
3. Measures for the economic development of underdeveloped countries; report by a group of experts
   appointed by the Secretary-General of the United
   Nations. New York (United Nations, Dep. of econ.
   affairs) 1951.
4. Commodity trade and economic development; submitted
   by a Committee appointed by the Secretary-General.
   New York (United Nations, Dep. of econ. affairs) 1953.

INTERNATIONAL TRADE
UNDER CONSTANT RETURNS IN A VERY
SIMPLE MODEL

In appendices 1 and 2 some basic theorems of the theory of international trade will be discussed for those who want to go into the rigorous theoretical foundations of our subject matter. The treatment, although exact, is very simple still and only represents an introduction to modern theory in two of its aspects. The mathematics used is mainly simple algebra and arithmetics in appendix 1 and graphical analysis in appendix 2. The theory of international trade is a vast body of theorems bearing on situations and problems which show many aspects. The discipline has grown rapidly in recent decades and the need for co-ordination becomes stronger and stronger. To the author it seems that four aspects in particular deserve attention since they profoundly influence the structure of the problems. These four aspects could be said to be:

(a) the 'monetary' aspect (M): is full employment (F) presupposed or is unemployment (U) accepted as a possibility?
(b) the 'technical' aspect (T): is production technology assumed to be rigid (R) or are the production factors assumed to be substitutable (S)?
(c) the nature of 'compartments' (C), i.e. the units of production considered: are they industries connected with groups of products (P) or representing only certain activities (A)? An example of the latter approach, rather

common in the theory of international trade, is the procedure which only considers the imports of finished products and combines imports of raw materials with the exports of the corresponding products; then only 'processing', an activity rather than a product, is made the basis of study.

(d) the number of 'compartments' (N): is there only one (1) per country, or more (j)?

Summarizing the aspects by the letter symbols indicated we may have

Aspects	M	T	C	N
Possible assumptions	F,U	R,S	P,A	1,j

A large number of combinations is possible and has in fact be dealt with by various theorists[1]. In our two appendices we will deal with two models which might both be characterized by the symbols:

$$F \quad R \quad A \quad 2$$

meaning that in both cases full employment will be assumed throughout, a rigid relation between input and output will

---

[1] Of some recent models the following characteristic may be given in our symbols:

P. A. Samuelson, 'International Trade and the Equalisation of Factor Prices', The Economic Journal LVIII (1948) p. 163 and subsequent discussion by J. Tinbergen and J. E. Meade in Metroeconomica: model F S A j.

M. Fleming, 'On Making the Best of Balance of Payments Restrictions on Imports, The Economic Journal 61 (1951) p. 48 and subsequent discussion by J. Tinbergen, 'Four Alternative Policies to Restore Balance of Payments Equilibrium', Econometrica 20 (1952) p. 372 and J. Tinbergen and H. M. A. van der Werff: model F R A 1(j).

F. Machlup, 'International Trade and the National Income Multiplier', Philadelphia, 1943, J. J. Polak, 'An International Economic System', London, 1954, and L. A. Metzler, 'A Multiplier-Region Theory of Income and Trade', Econometrica 18 (1950), p. 329: model U R P 1.

be supposed to exist, the nature of the compartments is that of activities (i.e. the imports of raw materials are disregarded as parts of imports) and there are two industries per country. The only difference is that in appendix 1 production processes are considered in which the relation between 'output' and factor input is a constant and the same for successive units of product ('constant returns'), whereas in appendix 2 this relation is variable, admitting 'decreasing' and 'increasing' returns. In appendix 1 a number of features are to be found which are characteristic for both classical theory and for modern 'linear programming', but in the simplest form conceivable. It may be an easy introduction to both and in particular also to Professor FRANK D. GRAHAM's 'Theory of International Values' (1948). In appendix 2 some use is made of indifference curves and production theory; it represents a generalization in some respects and a limitation in others (the influence of boundary conditions, very important in appendix 1, is almost disregarded, as was usual in neo-classical analysis).

From the foregoing remarks it will be clear how elementary the appendices are in comparison to the whole body of the theory of international trade. They do throw some light on the 'main thesis' of free trade theory, however, and may stimulate the reader to further study.

The model to be discussed first will use arithmetics and simple algebra. It is given for the case of *one factor* of production (labour), two countries 1 and 2 (upper indices) and *two products* 1 and 2 (lower indices), produced in two different industries, also indicated by these lower indices. It is assumed that the number of hours of labour a_j^i needed to produce, in country i one unit of product j

remains *unchanged* whatever the number of units produced. The four figures will be taken equal to

$$\begin{bmatrix} a_1^1 & a_2^1 \\ a_1^2 & a_2^2 \end{bmatrix} = \begin{bmatrix} 1 & 1.1 \\ 2.4 & 2 \end{bmatrix}$$

in our numerical examples.

Two types of situations will be considered: an *'open'* situation in which the two countries are in connection with a world market, large in comparison to their production, at which the two products have a price = 1. This model may be useful for the study of 'small countries'. A *'closed'* situation will also be considered, where only these two countries exist; here still one price, p_1, will be chosen equal to 1, since only relative prices matter in our problem.

The total number of workers in both countries, to be indicated by W^1 and W^2 is given (in our examples $W^1 = 10$, $W^2 = 20$) and it is assumed that they are always all of them employed. The number of workers in each 'compartment' (i.e. an industry in a country) will be indicated by w_j^i. Sometimes it will be assumed that there is only a *limited 'capacity to produce'* c_j^i in each compartment, i.e. that $w_j^i \leqq c_j^i$ is a condition imposed on the number of workers. The reason may be a limitation in some capital goods (with infinite life time and completely written off). It is assumed that there is *free competition* between employers leading to a wage rate l^i in each country which equals the marginal product of labour. The employers may not have any income at all as a consequence of this competition.

In the 'open' problems demand for the two products evidently is infinitely elastic; any quantity can be sold 'on the world market' that cannot be sold at home.

With the 'closed' problems this is different; it will be assumed that demand satisfies two conditions:

(i) total income is spent; no more, no less;

(ii) the ratio of the quantities demanded of both products is a function (equal in both countries) of the ratio of their prices. Indicating by:

p_1^i and p_2^i the prices in country i of products 1 and 2,

y_1^i and y_2^i the quantities produced,

x_1^i and x_2^i the quantities demanded,

we will have the following relations:

(a) Income equals expenditure:

$$y_1^1 p_1 + y_2^1 p_2 = x_1^1 p_1 + x_2^1 p_2 \qquad (1)$$

$$y_1^2 p_1 + y_2^2 p_2 = x_1^2 p_1 + x_2^2 p_2 \qquad (2)$$

(b) Supply equals demand:

$$y_1^1 + y_1^2 = x_1^1 + x_1^2 \qquad (3)$$

$$y_2^1 + y_2^2 = x_2^1 + x_2^2 \qquad (4)$$

It is well known that of these four equations, one is a consequence of the others; only three are independent.

(c) Relative demand a function of relative prices:

$$\frac{x_1^1}{x_2^1} = \frac{x_1^2}{x_2^2} = c \, \frac{p_2}{p_1} + c_0 \qquad (5), (6)$$

where c and c_0 are constants.

(d) Supply follows from number of workers:

$$y_1^1 = a_1^1 w_1^1 \qquad y_2^1 = a_2^1 w_2^1 \qquad (7), (8)$$

$$y_1^2 = a_1^2 w_1^2 \qquad y_2^2 = a_2^2 w_2^2 \qquad (9), (10)$$

(3) All workers are employed:

$$w_1^1 + w_2^1 = W^1 \qquad w_1^2 + w_2^2 = W^2 \qquad (11), (12)$$

Here it has been assumed that prices p_1^1 and p_1^2 of product 1 are equal in both countries, and p_2^1 and p_2^2 as well. Without import duties this is correct, since we neglect transportation costs.

If import duties are introduced, prices need not be equal any more in the two countries. We will use the symbols p_1 and p_2 to indicate 'world market prices' and equations (1) and (2) will still hold good, since they may be interpreted to indicate foreign exchanges only, if they are written in the form:

$$(y_1^i - x_1^i)p_1 + (y_2^i - x_2^i)p_2 = 0, \qquad i = 1,2,$$

where the expressions in parentheses represent net export surpluses.

Internal prices will now be influenced by import duties; indicating the duties levied as the ratio between the price inclusive of duty and the price exclusive of duty, and writing for this ratio τ_j^i we have:

$$\tau_j^i = \frac{p_j^i}{p_j} = \frac{p_j^i + t_j^i}{p_j}$$

where t_j^i represents the absolute value of the duty. Relative demand will now be different from what equations (5) and (6) indicate.

Import duties will be assumed to be levied only by country 1 on product 2 and by country 2 on product 1, since in our numerical example country 1 has a comparative advantage in producing product 1 and country 2 in producing product 2 and hence they will have to export these products if any. They could, of course, nevertheless impose an import duty on these products if they wanted to keep their prices above world market level inside their countries, but no such price discrimination between home market and exports will be assumed here.

Relative demand equations then become, if $\dfrac{p_2}{p_1} = \pi$:

$$\frac{x_1^1}{x_2^1} = c\,\pi\tau_2^1 + c_0 \qquad (5')$$

$$\frac{x_1^2}{x_2^2} = \frac{c\pi}{\tau_1^2} + c_0 \qquad (6')$$

The problems to be considered are the production and consumption patterns of both countries in the open as well as the closed situation, under conditions of free trade and protection. In particular the main thesis of free trade will be proved, that under free trade the value of production at free-trade prices will be larger than under protection. It will also be shown that this is not necessarily true of the value of expenditures at free-trade prices. We will discuss our subject matter by presenting a series of exactly defined partial problems.

PROBLEM 1: *open situation; no capacity limits; free trade*. World market prices are 1 for both products and are also prevailing inside both countries. Value created per hour will be equal to $1/a_j^i$ in each compartment. For country 1 it will be higher in industry 1 than in industry 2; wages will be bid up to $1/a_1^1 = 1$ and no workers can be employed in industry 2; wages will be, for the same reason, 0,5 in country 2 and no workers will be employed in industry 1. The production pattern will be:

$$\begin{bmatrix} y_1^1 & y_2^1 \\ y_1^2 & y_2^2 \end{bmatrix} = \begin{bmatrix} 10 & 0 \\ 0 & 10 \end{bmatrix}$$

and the employment pattern:

$$\begin{bmatrix} w^1_1 & w^{1'}_2 \\ w^2_1 & w^2_2 \end{bmatrix} = \begin{bmatrix} 10 & 0 \\ 0 & 20 \end{bmatrix}$$

The value of production will amount to 10 in either country.

PROBLEM 2: *open situation; capacity limits; free trade*. As an example we take capacity limits to be:

$$\begin{bmatrix} c^1_1 & c^{1'}_2 \\ c^2_1 & c^2_2 \end{bmatrix} = \begin{bmatrix} 7 & 5 \\ 13 & 9 \end{bmatrix}$$

Consequently, no more than 7 workers can be employed in industry 1 in country 1; the other 3 will have to be engaged in industry 2; the wage level will be $1/1.1 = 0.91$; in country 2, 9 workers will be employed in industry 2, the remaining 11 in industry 1 and the wage rate will be $1/2.4 = 0.42$. It appears that the capacities in the industries with a comparative advantage enter as additional boundary conditions into the problem. The capacities in the other industries would only do so if total capacity were insufficient to employ all workers.

This problem is mainly intended to illustrate that limited capacity may act as a brake on the adaptation process from, say, a state of protection (cf. problem 3) to a state of free trade (problem 1).

PROBLEM 3: *open situation; capacity limits; protection*. Suppose that for historical reasons (i.e. for reasons originating from the situation when transportation was much more expensive) a certain volume of production exists in the industries with comparative disadvantages. What import duties are needed to guarantee the continuation of this production? Let the capacity limits, which now have a different function from what it was in problem 2, be

$$c_1^1 = \infty \qquad c_2^1 = 6$$
$$c_1^2 = 8 \qquad c_2^2 = \infty$$

i.e. there is no limitation for c_1^1 and c_2^2. In order that 6 workers be indeed attracted by industry 2 in country 1 they must be offered a wage equal to the one in industry 1, which is 1; for the employer to be able to pay this wage, he has to receive a price p_2^1 of 1.1; an import duty of 0.1 will be needed. On similar grounds a duty of 0.2 will be needed in country 2 on product 1 (in order that its price be 1.2).

The value of production at free-trade prices will now amount to:

Country 1: $y_1^1 + y_2^1 = w_1^1 + \dfrac{w_2^1}{a_2^1} = 4 + \dfrac{6}{1.1} = 9\frac{5}{11}.$

Country 2: $y_1^2 + y_2^2 = \dfrac{w_1^2}{a_1^2} + \dfrac{w_2^2}{a_2^2} = \dfrac{8}{2.4} + \dfrac{12}{2} = 9\frac{1}{3}.$

It will be easily understood that this is, for both countries, less than the value 10 found in problem 1, as long as production is partly going on in the industries with a comparative disadvantage.

PROBLEM 4: *closed situation; no capacity limits; free trade.* As set out before, the demand side will now have to be brought in. It evidently depends on the numerical values of the coefficients c and c_0 what the ratio of quantities demanded will be. It seems useful to consider the various cases that may present themselves. Depending on the relative price level $\pi = \frac{p_2}{p_1}$ various production patterns may result. Each country may either produce both products or it may 'specialize' on one. For both products to be produced simultaneously, π has to be equal to the ratio $\frac{a_2^i}{a_1^i}$; only product 2 will be produced if π surpasses this ratio and only product 1 will be produced if π is below it. Since the ratio is 1.1 for country 1 and 0.83 for country 2, the following cases would seem possible, where an asterisk indicates production and a zero no production:

Case	Value of π	Country 1		Country 2	
		Prod. 1	Prod. 2	Prod. 1	Prod. 2
1	$\pi < 0.83$	*	o	*	o
2	$\pi = 0.83$	*	o	*	*
3	$0.83 < \pi < 1.1$	*	o	o	*
4	$\pi = 1.1$	*	*	o	*
5	$\pi > 1.1$	o	*	o	*

Upon closer consideration it will be clear, however, that cases 1 and 5 have to be excluded, since, in a closed situation, it is evidently impossible to satisfy the equilibrium conditions if one of the commodities is not produced at all.

Another conclusion following from our table is that with $\frac{a_2^1}{a_1^1} \neq \frac{a_2^2}{a_1^2}$ one country at least has to specialize. Since π is not given beforehand, but follows from the equilibrium conditions expressed in equations (1) – (12), we have to solve these equations before knowing which of the cases applies. The logical structure of our problem is that c and c_0 are

166

given and the x's, w's, y's and π unknowns, whereas the relation between π and the w's or y's is of the discontinuous character disclosed by the last table. Mathematically it will be simpler to assume π to be given and deduce the values for c and c_0.

Taking case 2, i.e. $w_2^1 = y_2^1 = 0$, we have, e.g.: $w_1^1 = W^1 = 10$; equations (1) – (6) become:

$$10 + 0 = (0.83\,c + c_0 + 0.83)\,x_2^1$$

$$\frac{20 - w_2^2}{2.4} + \frac{w_2^2}{2}\,0.83 = (0.83\,c + c_0 + 0.83)\,x_2^2$$

$$\frac{w_2^2}{2} = x_2^1 + x_2^2$$

or:

$$x_2^1 = \frac{10}{0.83\,(c+1) + c_0} \qquad x_2^2 = \frac{20}{2\,(c+1) + 2.4\,c_0}$$

$$w_2^2 = \frac{44}{c + 1 + 1.2\,c_0}$$

It follows that for $c + 1 + 1.2\,c_0 \gtreqless 2.2$, $w_2^2 \lesseqgtr 20$. If, therefore, $c + 1.2\,c_0 = 1.2$, the demand for good 2 would be so strong as to equal country 2's productive capacity and a situation would come into existence where the country would have to specialize on product 2. The formulae would no longer be valid, and hence are only so for

$$c + 1.2\,c_0 \geq 1.2 \tag{13}$$

By equal methods we find that for case 3 to apply c and c_0 have to satisfy:

$$0.91\,(1 - c_0) < c < 1.2\,(1 - c_0) \tag{14}$$

167

It may be observed that the right-hand boundary condition here expressed co-incides with the one implied in (13).

For case 4: $1.1c + c_0 \leqq 1$ (15)

We are now able to invert our findings, according to the logical structure of the problem and may summarize the situation for problem 4 as follows:

$0.91(1-c_0) \geqq c$	$0.91(1-c_0) < c < 1.2(1-c_0)$	$c \geqq 1.2(1-c_0)$
$\pi = 1.1$ $w_1^2 = y_1^2 = 0$ $w_2^1 = \dfrac{10-11c+10c_0}{1+c+0.91c_0}$	$1.1 > \pi > 0.83$ $w_1^2 = w_2^1 = y_1^2 = y_2^1 = 0$	$\pi = 0.83$ $w_2^1 = y_2^1 = 0$ $w_2^2 = \dfrac{44}{1+c+1.2c_0}$

For our further examples we choose $c_0 = 0$, $c = 1.5$, leading to:

$$\begin{bmatrix} y_1^1 & y_2^1 \\ y_1^2 & y_2^2 \end{bmatrix} = \begin{bmatrix} 10 & 0 \\ 1 & 8.8 \end{bmatrix}; \begin{bmatrix} x_1^1 & x_2^1 \\ x_1^2 & x_2^2 \end{bmatrix} = \begin{bmatrix} 6 & 4.8 \\ 5 & 4 \end{bmatrix}$$

At free-trade prices, i.e. at the prices prevailing with this c_0 and c, or $\pi = 0.83$, the value of production equals, for country 1: 10 and for country 2: 8.33. These values are equal to the values of expenditure, as is easily tested.

PROBLEM 5: *closed situation; no capacity limits; protection.* The logical structure of this problem is very similar to the one of problem 4; in addition to c_0 and c, the import duties τ_2^1 and τ_1^2 are also given. Since they are able to change the price ratios inside the countries, there are also several possibilities as to the production pattern, depending on these data. In order not to make our argument too complicated we take the numerical values of c_0 and c chosen in problem 4, namely $c_0 = 0$, $c = 1.5$. The number of cases possible under protection is larger, since e.g. simultaneous production of both commodities in both countries is now possible. Since the object of protection is, in many cases, to maintain such a production pattern, we will even take this very case as our special numerical example. Before considering this we may first give a survey of all possible cases. This may be given the following tabular form:

	$\pi\tau_2^1 < \dfrac{a_2^1}{a_1^1}$	$\pi\tau_2^1 = \dfrac{a_2^1}{a_1^1}$	$\pi\tau_2^1 > \dfrac{a_2^1}{a_1^1}$
$\dfrac{\pi}{\tau_1^2} < \dfrac{a_2^2}{a_1^2}$	(1) Impossible	(2) $w_2^2 = 0$	(3) $w_1^1 = w_2^2 = 0$
$\dfrac{\pi}{\tau_1^2} = \dfrac{a_2^2}{a_1^2}$	(4) $w_2^1 = 0$	(5) All $w \neq 0$	(6) $w_1^1 = 0$
$\dfrac{\pi}{\tau_1^2} > \dfrac{a_2^2}{a_1^2}$	(7) $w_1^1 = w_1^2 = 0$	(8) $w_1^2 = 0$	(9) Impossible

It appears from the table that in cases of very high duties (case (3)), even anti-specialization would be possible; in cases of low tariffs a tendency towards normal specialization (case (7)) may still exist. Cases (1) and (9) are again impossible because both countries would specialize on the same product. The case we are going to consider is case (5), for which we have the condition $\tau_2^1 \, \tau_1^2 = \dfrac{a_2^1 a_1^2}{a_1^1 a_2^2}$. Although it may seem 'improbable' that such a condition would be fulfilled by chance, it should not be overlooked that often, as observed already, this case is the very situation aimed at.

Mathematically the case has the attractive feature that equations $(5')$ and $(6')$, which have now to be substituted for (5) and (6), reduce to equations without π, namely:

$$x_1^1 = 1.65\, x_2^1$$
$$x_1^2 = 1.25\, x_2^2$$

Furthermore it appears that there is still a double infinity of cases fulfilling our condition; for we are left with 7 independent equations between 9 variables (4 x's, 4 y's and π), these equations being equations $(1) - (12)$, after elimination, with the aid of $(7) - (10)$, the four w's and leaving out one of the first four $(1) - (4)$. The double infinity of cases evidently corresponds with the freedom in both countries which employers have, under the circumstances specified, to produce either good 1 or good 2. By every choice they make all the other variables, including π, determined. In the case without protection such a freedom does not exist, even in the one country in which, in cases 2 and 4 of problem 4, simultaneous production in two industries occurs. For here any choice as to the production pattern determines not only π, the price ratio on the world market, but at the same time the price ratio inside each country. In our present problem, where we took $\pi \tau_2^1$ and $\dfrac{\pi}{\tau_1^2}$ as given, import duties are assumed to be so manipulated as to keep these internal price ratios at the values assumed.

Since we are only interested in an example, and not primarily in the complete solution of all cases implied, we have chosen deliberately among the double infinity of possible solutions. This we have done, firstly, by choosing π rather than one of the y's, and, secondly by choosing one of the y's. Our choice has been $\pi = 1$ and $y_1^2 = 2$. With the latter choice we have taken care not to choose a value — which would have been possible — leading to a negative value for one of the other y's. The following values appear to satisfy all our equations (1) – (4), (5'), (6'), (7) – (12):

$$\begin{bmatrix} y_1^1 & y_2^1 \\ y_1^2 & y_2^2 \end{bmatrix} = \begin{bmatrix} 9.25 & 0.43 \\ 2.00 & 7.60 \end{bmatrix}; \quad \begin{bmatrix} x_1^1 & x_2^1 \\ x_1^2 & x_2^2 \end{bmatrix} = \begin{bmatrix} 6.20 & 3.76 \\ 5.32 & 4.28 \end{bmatrix}$$

With their help we may now calculate the values of production and expenditure both at current world-market prices and at free-trade prices (i.e. at the prices prevailing in problem 4). For comparison we repeat the values found in problem 4 and summarize all results in the table below:

Value of:	At prices:	Free trade		Protection	
		Countries: 1	2	1	2
Production	Current	10.00	8.33	9.96	9.60
Expenditure	Current	10.00	8.33	9.96	9.60
Production	Free-trade	10.00	8.33	9.88	8.31
Expenditure	Free-trade	10.00	8.33	9.32	8.37

It appears, of course, that production value and expenditure are equal to each other, in each country, for current prices, which in the case of free trade are at the same time free-trade prices. They are not necessarily equal in the case of protection when valued at free-trade prices. The divergencies then reflect the influence exerted by a change in the terms of trade as compared with free trade. In our example, country 1 suffers a loss by this change, country 2 shows a gain. For both countries the value of production at free-trade prices has decreased from free trade to protection and so, evidently, has total production value for both countries together, and consequently, total value of expenditure for both countries together. This applies not only to our example, but would have been found to be true for any example within our model. What our example proves, in addition, is the possibility that, under protection, one country may gain on the free-trade value of its expenditure; in fact, country 2 does. This is an illustration of two important principles, namely

(i) that the central thesis of free-trade theory cannot be proved, under the assumptions made, for any welfare concept; and

(ii) that tariffs may be used to manipulate, to the advantage of one country at least, the terms of trade in such a way as to increase the free-trade value of expenditure.

Finally it should be observed that the gain of country 2 could have been made available to that country in the case of free trade out of the larger gain in total production value for the two countries together under free trade, i.e. under free trade, total production might have been distributed between countries 1 and 2 so as to yield 8.87 to country 2 (as under protection) and leave to country 1 an amount of 9.49, which is still superior to what that country would have under protection (9.32). This is an application of the so-called 'compensation principle' of welfare economics.

INTERNATIONAL TRADE
UNDER VARIABLE RETURNS IN A VERY
SIMPLE MODEL[1]

After having discussed some problems of international trade for a two-country two-commodity model under constant returns we will now deal with some problems under conditions of variable returns (i.e. decreasing as well as increasing returns). These problems will be under what conditions a country will have an advantage of international trade. Since only a comparison will be made between the situation without international trade and the situation with fully free international trade, no conclusions are drawn about any intermediary situations, e.g. situations with tariffs.

I. MEASURING THE 'ADVANTAGE' TO A COUNTRY OF INTERNATIONAL TRADE

Strictly speaking it is not possible to tell whether or not a given country has an 'advantage' from the existence of international trade, since it is, on closer examination, not possible to give a precise meaning to the notion of 'advantage' to a country. It is possible to speak of an advantage to a single person; a given change in his situation brings

---

[1] This appendix forms the largest part of Appendix 1 in the first edition of this book (under the title 'International Economic Co-operation'). I have omitted the discussion with Professor Frank D. Graham since I did not arrive at different conclusions, but only doubted whether his numerical example was consistent.

him either to a higher or to a lower level of satisfaction (ophelimity). Since this satisfaction cannot be measured and, a fortiori, a common measure for the satisfaction of the various subjects constituting a country does not exist, it is, however, impossible to add up the advantages or disadvantages for the single persons and hence also to give a precise meaning to the notion of advantage to a country. As, on the other hand, the discussion on the 'advantages of international trade' only has sense if some convention on this notion is accepted, we shall, in what follows, proceed as if a country as a whole also possesses a system of 'indifference curves', similar to those for a single person. We speak of 'curves' only and not of surface, etc., since we shall only discuss cases in which we have to do with two commodities 1 and 2, the consumed quantities of which, x_1' and x_2', determine the 'satisfaction' of the country $\Omega\ (x_1',\ x_2')$. Each indifference curve $\Omega\ (x_1',\ x_2') = C$ is constituted of (is the locus of) all commodity combinations x_1', x_2', that yield an equal satisfaction to a country. A combination x_1'', x_2'' yielding a higher satisfaction than a combination is situated on a 'higher indifference curve' etc. We make the usual assumption that these curves turn their convex side to the origin.

2. THE POSSIBILITY OF DECREASING AND INCREASING MARGINAL COST

For simplicity's sake we assume that there is only one productive agent, which we call labour. The total quantity of labour a is given and is fully employed. The quantities used in the production of commodities 1 and 2 are denoted by a_1 and a_2; hence

$$a_1 + a_2 = a \qquad (1)$$

The quantity a_1 depends on the quantity x_1 of commodity 1 it is desired to produce; likewise a_2 depends on x_2:

$$a_1 = \varphi_1(x_1) \qquad (2)$$

$$a_2 = \varphi_2(x_2) \qquad (3)$$

The functions φ_1 and φ_2 are called *cost functions*. Marginal cost in each case is $\varphi_1'(x_1)$ and $\varphi_2'(x_2)$, respectively; these expressions always have positive values. They may, however, be increasing or decreasing functions of x_1 and x_2. The case of *increasing marginal cost* is the normal case. *Decreasing marginal cost* for a whole branch of industry will hardly occur. Even if for a single enterprise the 'law of decreasing marginal cost' is assumed to prevail, it need not be valid for the industry as a whole. The law will, as a rule, only exist for certain intervals of the quantity produced in a single enterprise. It is a well-known fact that no situation of competitive equilibrium is possible within such an interval. If the branch is constituted of more that one enterprise, an extension of production will usually mean the necessity of using less productive units, i.e. increasing marginal cost. Only if the most economic size of the unit exceeds the size of the branch as a whole, will there be one enterprise; then, too, competitive equilibrium within the interval of decreasing marginal cost is not possible.

3. A GRAPHICAL REPRESENTATION OF THE EQUILIBRIUM OF PRODUCTION AND INTERNATIONAL TRADE

In fig. 1 let x_1 and x_1' be measured along the positive part of the horizontal axis and x_2 and x_2' along the positive part of the vertical axis. The negative halves of these axes are used for plotting a_1 and a_2, respectively. In the fourth quadrant we draw the cost curve $a_1 = \varphi_1(x_1)$, assumed to be of the normal (convex) type. In the second quadrant the curve $a_2 = \varphi_2(x_2)$ is drawn in a similar way; to begin with, it is also assumed to be convex. In the third quadrant the line $a_1 + a_2 = a$ is indicated, being the locus of all possible applications of productive resources. From these data the *'production curve'* may be deduced, indicating all combinations x_1, x_2 that the country is able to produce. This curve has the equation:

$$\varphi_1(x_1) + \varphi_2(x_2) = a \qquad (4)$$

Any point Q of this curve is obtained from the corre-

Fig 1

sponding point Q' of the line (1) by the dotted lines in fig. 1. In the absence of international trade quantities produced x_1, and x_2 coincide with quantities consumed x_1' and x_2'. For its consumption the country therefore has to choose between the points on the production curve only. It will attain maximum satisfaction if it chooses point A where the production curve is tangent to one of the ophelimity curves, plotted against the x_1-x_2-axes: there is no point with a higher satisfaction to be found on the production curve. Under free competition this point will be attained automatically. The price relation between goods 1 and 2 will be indicated by the absolute value of the slope

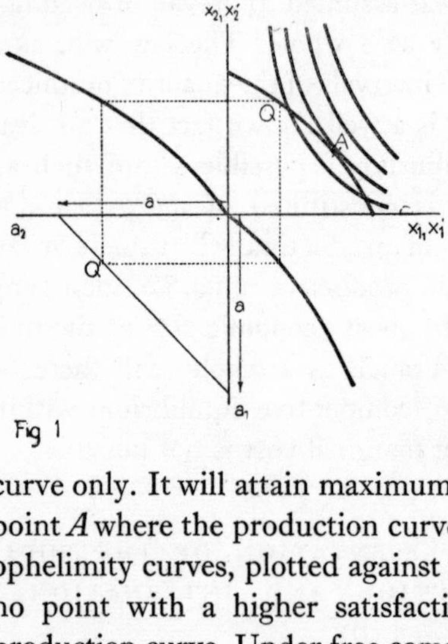

176

of the common tangent line to the two curves in A; i.e. that slope indicates the ratio between the quantity of x_2 exchanged for a unit of x_1; i.e. the price of x_1 in terms of x_2.

Now assume that an opportunity is opened to buy or sell in an international market at a given price p of x_1 in terms of x_2, represented graphically by the slope of the line RS in fig. 2, where the first quadrant of fig. 1 has been reproduced. This means, first, that no longer x_1 has to coincide with x_1' and x_2 with x_2'.

A 'consumption point' $x_1'\ x_2'$ may now be reached, different from the 'production point' $x_1\ x_2$ and connected with the latter by the equation

$$x_1' = x_1 + \frac{1}{p}(x_2 - x_2'), \qquad (5)$$

indicating that the consumption of good 1 equals its production x_1, plus the quantity bought in the international market, at a price p, for a quantity $x_2 - x_2'$ of good 2; the consumption of 2 now being less than x_2. Of course also x_2' may be $>x_2$, but then x_1' will be $<x_1$.

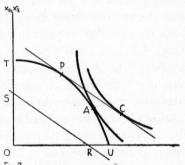

Fig 2

Fig. 2 easily discloses what the new equilibrium situation will be. With the given price relation p producers will find it advantageous to use their productive resources in another way than before: in the case assumed in fig. 2, where p is lower than the price relation prevailing at point A, it will pay them to produce more of good 2 and less of good 1; equilibrium will be attained only if the marginal products obtained are of equal value. This means that they will proceed to point P, where the tangent line to the production curve is parallel to the given line $R\,S$. Having produced the quantities x_1, x_2, corresponding with P, the country is now free to exchange part of its production at the terms expressed in equation (5), i.e., in graphical language, it is free to move along the 'price line' $P\,C$. This it will do until it has reached the point of maximum satisfaction, being point C, where $P\,C$ is tangent to an indifference curve. The new equilibrium is therefore represented by the two points P, C, the *production* and the *consumption point*, respectively.

Under conditions later to be enumerated, *the satisfaction obtained in the new situation will always be greater than that obtained in the old one*. For $P\,C$, as a tangent to a convex curve, will, for any value of x_1, show a higher value of x_2 than the corresponding point of the production curve[1]. Since the equilibrium point in the absence of international trade, A, is necessarily a point of the production curve, the satisfaction in C always exceeds that in A, except in the particular case where A and C coincide, i.e. where the price relation p in the world market equals the price relation existing without international trade. Hence, under the conditions to be discussed, *the introduction of international trade always means an advantage* to a country; with the exception of such 'boundary cases' where the advantage is zero.

---

[1] From P to the left, $\dfrac{dx_2}{dx_1}$ for the production curve is, in absolute measure, always smaller than $\left|\dfrac{dx_2}{dx_1}\right|$ for the price line; from P to the right $\left|\dfrac{dx_2}{dx_1}\right|$ for the production curve is always larger than $\left|\dfrac{dx_2}{dx_1}\right|$ for the price line.

178

4. NON-TANGENT PRICE LINE

This important conclusion was reached on a number of conditions, the influence of which we will investigate in the following sections. The conditions are:
 (i) the production curve is convex;
 (ii) prices are equal to marginal costs;
(iii) there exists a point P on the production curve for which the slope of the tangent equals the price relation p in the world market.

We shall first remove the last condition. It is conceivable, in fact, that the price prevailing in the world market is lower or higher than the absolute value of the slope of any tangent to the production curve; in the case of a convex curve this only means that it is lower than that slope for T or higher than that for U, the two terminal points of the production curve. In those cases the production point will coincide with T or U respectively; the conclusions drawn remain valid, however, as is easily read from the diagram.

5. CONCAVE PRODUCTION CURVE

Next we remove the first condition mentioned in section 4. This condition is closely connected with the nature of the cost curves assumed. If both cost curves are of the increasing marginal cost type, the production curve is convex. It may be convex too, however, if one of the cost curves is of another type. This depends on the degree in which the curve deviates from the normal type. We shall go into this question in section 6 below. Now we start from the other end and we assume that both cost curves are decreasing marginal cost curves. Graphically, this means

179

that both these curves are themselves concave and it easily
follows that also the production curve is concave (fig. 3).
Now all points on the production curve, except the terminal
points, are *unstable equilibria*. Extension of the production
of one of the goods at the expense of the other always
means an increase in total value of production: the ex-
panding industry gets more productive and the declining
industry less productive than at the initial point.

If the opportunity of international trading is opened at a
price ratio corresponding to the slope of a line $T V$, point
T will be the more advantageous point and similar to
what we discussed above (section 3) a consumption point C

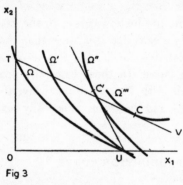

Fig 3

will be chosen. General-
ly point T will, in the
presence of trading op-
portunities, be the pro-
duction point if the
price of 1 in terms of 2
is lower than the figure
corresponding with the
line $T U$, whereas U
will be the production
point if that price is
higher than that figure. As an example of this latter
situation, the price line $U C'$ is drawn, with a consumption point C'.

Again the conclusion can be drawn that the *introduction
of international trade increases the satisfaction to be obtained
for the country*, with the exception of possible (but not
necessarily existing) boundary cases. One boundary case
is the one where the price line through U coincides with the
tangent to the ophelimity curve through that point (Ω').

6. A STRAIGHT LINE AS PRODUCTION CURVE; MIXED CASES

As a special case, often made use of in simple expositions of the theory of international trade (cf. appendix 1), we now consider the case where the cost curves are straight lines, the case of *constant marginal costs*. The production curve is now a straight line too, of which each point is a point of indifferent equilibrium. Apart from this difference with the preceding case the same conclusions are valid. More complications arise if one of the industries operates under increasing and the other under decreasing marginal costs. It then depends on the exact form of the two cost curves, whether the production curve is convex, concave or of a more complicated type. If one cost curve is 'highly' convex and the other only 'slightly'

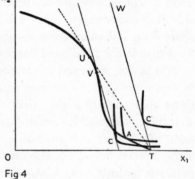

Fig 4

concave, the production curve will be convex, etc. There may be intervals where convexity and others where concavity prevails[1].

---

[1] A more exact study must be based on the analytical expression for these properties. An interval of a curve $y = f(x)$ is convex if $\dfrac{d^2y}{dx^2} < 0$ throughout that interval. In the notations used above we have:

$$\frac{d^2x_2}{dx_1^2} = \frac{\dfrac{d^2\varphi_2}{da_2^2} + \dfrac{d\varphi_1}{da_1} \cdot \dfrac{d\varphi_2}{da_2} \Big/ \dfrac{d\varphi_1}{da_1}}{\left(\dfrac{d\varphi_1}{da_1}\right)^2} = \frac{\varphi_2'' + \varphi_1'' \dfrac{\varphi_2'}{\varphi_1'}}{\varphi_1'^2} \qquad (6)$$

In order to suggest that also in these cases of a 'mixed' production curve our statement about the advantage of international trade holds as a rule, we consider an arbitrary case of this class (cf. fig. 4).

For prices lower than the slope of $T U$ a stable production equilibrium will be found between U and S. The consumption point will be either at the exterior of the production curve or, in boundary cases, on that curve. Therefore, the satisfaction will be at least as great as before the existence of international trade.

For prices higher than corresponds to the slope of $T U$, point T will be one possible production point. The corresponding consumption point will lie on $T U$ and hence — apart from boundary cases — show a higher satisfaction level than in the absence of international trade.

This is not, however, the whole story. For some prices in this interval there are two equilibrium points. With a price only slightly higher than that corresponding with $T U$ there is a possible equilibrium point in the neighbourhood of U, since the production curve is convex also for some interval below U. The existence of two equilibrium points is nothing new: it was discussed in some detail by Koopmans[1]. It implies that, if by trial and error over small

Since φ_2' and φ_1' are always positive, we see that $\dfrac{d^2x_2}{dx_1^2}$ is a weighted sum of φ_2'' and φ_1''; the weights varying along the curve. If φ_2'' and φ_1'' are of equal sign, $\dfrac{d^2x_2}{dx_1^2}$ has the same sign; if they are, however, of opposite sign, many possibilities exist.

[1] J. G. Koopmans, 'De mogelijkheid van meervoudig economisch evenwicht', De Economist *81* (1932), p. 679, 766 and 841 and 'Marginale kosten, marginale opbrengsten en optimale productie-omvang' in: Economische opstellen aangeboden aan Prof. Mr F. de Vries, Haarlem 1944, p. 149.

distances of the production curve, one of these equilibrium points is found and persists, the possibility exists that this point is not the absolute optimum but only a relative one. If we assume complete knowledge of all data with the economic subjects, they finally will choose the absolute optimum.

If that knowledge is not supposed to exist, they may stay at the lower, relative, maximum. In that latter case it may happen that the consumption point is one of lower satisfaction than the one prevailing before international trade was introduced. This case occurs if the course of the ophelimity curves happens to be such that the tangent points lies below W (cf. fig. 4). It then lies in the interior of the production curve.

Hence, *one condition has to be maintained in these mixed cases: the one of perfect market knowledge.*

7. CALCULATION OF PRICES ON THE BASIS OF AVERAGE INSTEAD OF MARGINAL COST

Finally we have to investigate the consequence of a removal of condition (ii) (section 4). This will appear to be a more serious threat to the validity of our statement. The necessity of assuming that prices are not equal to marginal costs of production only exists in the case of a decreasing marginal cost function. In industries where this law is valid, the equality of prices and marginal cost would entail a permanent loss to the producers. Hence it is probable that, in the long run, prices will be higher and in fact equal to average cost. In order to study the consequences of this hypothesis let us assume that industry 1 operates at decreasing marginal cost and that production is adjusted to its price in such a way as to make average cost equal to price. Since average costs are higher than marginal cost, this means that the (absolute value of the) slope of the price line is now, in the equilibrium point, higher than the slope of the tangent.

Let us further assume that the production curve is still convex. As the equilibrium point without international trade a point A will now be chosen where there is no longer identity of tangents to the production curve and the

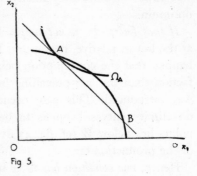

Fig 5

ophelimity curve. The price line $A B$ now intersects the production curve, since its slope must be higher than that of the tangent. It is still a tangent to the ophelimity curve.

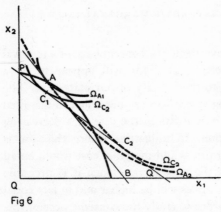

Fig 6

This already means that the point of maximum satisfaction on the production line is not chosen: this way of calculating prices is disadvantageous to the country (cf. fig. 5).

Now consider the case with international trade (fig. 6). Let $P Q$ be the price line and P the corresponding production point. There are two possibilities now, indicated in

184

fig. 6 by the subscripts 1 and 2 and by full and dotted ophelimity curves respectively. In the first case, where the ophelimity curve through A, Ω_{A1}, does not intersect with $P\,Q$, the consumption point C_1 shows indeed a lower degree of satisfaction than A. Here *international trade is a disadvantage to the country*. In the second case, where the ophelimity curve through A, Ω_{A2}, does intersect with $P\,Q$, the satisfaction in C_2 is again higher than that in A and our former statement remains valid. Since both possibilities must be recognized it follows that the removal of condition (ii) (section 4) is vital to our statement. Hence our general conclusions may be formulated: *in the simple case considered (two commodities and one agent of production) international trade is an advantage (or as a boundary case no disadvantage) to every country involved, provided that:*
1. there is perfect knowledge of market data and
2. prices are calculated on the basis of marginal cost.

8. A DIAGRAM FOR TWO COUNTRIES

So far we only considered the position of one country finding itself vis-à-vis a world market with a *given price relation p* for good 1 in terms of good 2. We shall now try to answer the question *how that relation* itself is determined in the simplified case where there is only one other country in that 'world' market. It is by a simple extension of our graphical method that the answer may be given. In fig. 7, relating, as far as our first country, 'country A', is concerned, to the same situation as fig. 2, the co-ordinates x_1, x_2, x'_1 and x'_2 are, as before, plotted from the origin O. The corresponding co-ordinates for country B, denoted by y_1, y_2, y'_1 and y'_2, are plotted from O', but in the opposite direction. The point O' is simply chosen in such a way that its co-ordinates with respect to O are $x_1 + y_1$ and $x_2 + y_2$, respectively, or, which is the same, $x'_1 + y'_1$ and $x'_2 + y'_2$. This implies that A's and B's production points coincide (point P) and their consumption points as well (C). A's ophelimity curves are indicated by — . — . —, whereas B's are indicated by — — — — curves. The point A and B are the production (and consumption) points of countries A and B respectively, in the absence of international trade. The essence of the graphical representation is that $P\,C$ is at the same time tangent to both production curves in P

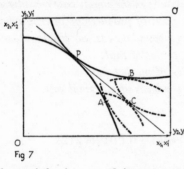

Fig 7

and to an ophelimity curve of each country in C. For the case represented, the one of convex production curves and point P for neither country in a 'boundary situation', the advantage of international trade to both countries is clear: the satisfaction to A is greater in C than in A and the satisfaction to B is greater in C than in B. The diagram cannot be constructed unless the position of C is given and this depends on the unknowns of the problem, namely x_1, x_2, y_1 and y_2. Hence it might seem that the diagram is of no help in finding p. As a matter of fact, all these unknowns must be determined simultaneously; i.e. one must so long 'play round' with O' until a position is found where there exists — which is not generally the case — a common double tangent line to the system of ophelimity curves and the two production curves.

There are a great number of different cases as to the

shape of the production curves and the situation of the production and consumption points; quite a number of boundary cases being among them. It may be left to the reader to go into these questions.

INDEX

Abilities of population, 31
Absolute scarcity of capital, 137
Agreements, commodity, 118
Aims of economic policy, 101
Austerity policy, 92

Balance of payments, 66
Balancing item, 67
Bank, International, 151
Bilateralism, 44
Budget, common, 140, 151
Budget, international investment, 140, 151

Capital per head, 35, 137
Capital movements, 62ff., 130
Centralization, 97, 99, 113, 142
Circular flows, 44
CLARK, COLIN, 33
Clearing, 74
Climate, social, 31, 38
Closed flows, 44
Coal and Steel Community, European, 121, 124
Colombo Plan, 151, 154
Commodity agreements, 118
Comparative cost, 54
Conflicting instruments, 99, 144
Convertibility, 81, 134
Critical elasticities, 91
Currency restrictions, 48, 78
Currency, world, 126
Current transactions, 40, 67
Customs union, 50, 59, 123

Decentralization, 97, 99
Deflationary gap, 84, 114, 151
Devaluation, 73
Development, 136 ff.
Discount rate, 71
Distance in international trade, 43

Distribution of income, 38, 55
Division of labour, international, 52, 116
Donations, 68
Duties, import, 48, 115, 117

Economic and Social Council, 149
Economic union, 50
EKKER, M. H., 74
Elasticities, critical, 91
Employment, high and stable, 85, 108
Equilibrium, formal vs material in balance of payments, 68
Equilibrium, monetary, 84
European Coal and Steel Community, 121, 124
European Payments Union, 133, 149
European Recovery Plan, 133, 154
Exchange equalization fund, 75
Exchange rate, 66, 111, 128
Exchange rate, stability of, 69

Factors of production, 32, 60
Family planning, 62, 138, 152
Financial policy, 110, 150
Financial transactions, 66 ff.
Financing, inflationary, 109
Flexible exchange rates, 75
Food and Agricultural Organization, 147
Free competition, 51
Free trade, 50
Free trade, doctrine of, 54
Free-trade area, 50
Full use of resources, 56

Gap, inflationary or deflationary, 84, 114, 151

General Agreement on Trade and Tariffs, 146
Gold, 66
Gold points, 70
Gold standard, 69

Half-capitalistic countries, 32
Hard currencies, 78
Harmonized policy, 142
HARTOG, F., 46
High-capitalistic countries, 32

Imperfect competition, 51
Incomes of countries, 34, 35
Inconvertibility, 73
Infant industry, 58
Inflation, 76, 87
Inflationary financing, 109
Inflationary gap, 84, 114, 151
Instruments of economic policy, 96
Instruments, conflicting, 99, 144
Instruments, mixed, 99
Instruments, neutral, 99
Instruments, supporting, 98
Integration, 30, 95, 106
Integration, positive, 122, 145
Integration, regional, 151
International Bank, 151
International Monetary Fund, 129, 148
International Trade Organization, 146

Land per head, 35, 36
Land, movements of, 60
Liberalization of trade, 58, 119, 146
Liquidity, degrees of, 131

Marginal-cost pricing, 55, 56
Marshall Plan, 133, 154
Migration, 61, 152

Mixed instruments, 99
Monetary equilibrium, 84
Monetary Fund, International, 129, 148
Multilateralism, 43, 50, 77

Net position, 46
Network of flows, 44
Neutral instruments, 99
New-capitalistic countries, 32
Non-capitalistic countries, 32

Objectives of economic policy, 101
O.E.E.C., 48, 133, 146
Open flows, 44
Optimum policy, 57, 95
Optimum population, 37
Optimum tariff, 56

Parity, 70
Point Four Program, 152
Policy, economic, 95
Population, 31
Price stabilization, 118
Product, national, 33

Qualitative policy, 96
Quantitative policy, 96
Quantitative restrictions, 48, 117, 121, 146
Quotes, 48

Raw Materials Conference, 147
Raw material standard, 75, 119
Regional integration, 151
Reserve, 74

SARGENT, J. R., 79
Soft currencies, 78
Special U. N. Fund for E. D., 152
Sterling Area, 79, 149
Sterling balances, 132

Subsidies, 115, 120
Subventions, 115, 120
Supporting instruments, 98

Targets of economic policy, 101
Tariff, optimum, 55
Tax policy, 110
Technical Assistance, 152
Terms of trade, 55
Tin Study Group, International-
al, 147
Trade-creating elements, 59
Trade-diverting elements, 59
Trade Organization, Interna-
tional 146
Transfer, 66
Transferability of sterling, 79

Unilateral payments, 67
Union, customs, 50, 59
Union, economic, 50
United Nations, 145
Units, international, 33

VERDOORN, P. J., 123
VINER, J., 59

WAGEMANN, 32
Wage policy, 111, 129
Wealth, 31
Wealth, natural, 31
Wheat Agreement, 147
World Bank, 151
World currency, 126